ব্রিক লেন

First published in the UK in 2018 by Kitchen Press Ltd.

1 Windsor Place
Dundee
DD2 1BG

Cover design by Sam Paton at Kin Studio.
Interior design and typesetting by Andrew Forteath.

A CIP catalogue record for this book is available from the British Library.

ISBN 9780957037397

Printed and bound in the UK by Bell & Bain Ltd.

FOR MY DEAREST NANI:

YOU ARE A LEGEND.

ACKNOWLEDGEMENTS

To my publisher Kitchen Press and Emily for taking a chance on me and helping to turn my passionate ramblings into a cookbook I'm proud to call my own. This project has been a labour of love in the best possible way, connecting my childhood memories to the vibrant present of a much loved area.

To my friends: Kia for her unwavering support and for always believing in me, Peter for agreeing to take beautiful photographs that capture the food and the essence of Brick Lane, Victoria for her expert recipe testing and for being my foodie partner in crime. Thank you all for cheering me on.

To my family: most importantly my mother for her culinary magic, tips on recipes and techniques and for answering my endless questions. Thanks also to my sister Jorna for helping with my food photoshoot prep, especially when rescuing bundt cakes in the middle of the night. I know how you all endure my non-stop food talk. There's more to come.

Finally, I am grateful to Uncle Roger for his support and literary wisdom. Thank you for encouraging me to kick-start my cookbook journey and always reading my writing.

POWER LEAGUE
POWERLEA
SHOREDITC
• 11 x 5-a-side pitches • 2
ther & floodlit
• Kids' parti
• Corpor
SHORE ITCH STATION
30

INTRODUCTION
DINA BEGUM

MY LOVE AFFAIR WITH BRICK LANE STARTED IN THE MARKET. I'VE ALWAYS LOVED THE HUSTLE AND BUSTLE OF TRADERS DISPLAYING THEIR WARES, OFFERING SAMPLES, ENTICING YOU IN WITH VOICES SOFT AND LOUD, PUNCTUATED BY THE LILT OF GLOBAL ACCENTS.

As a child in the 1980s I would visit the Sunday market with my dad, fascinated by the many types of stalls set up in the road. There were stalls selling second-hand furniture, jewellery, bric-a-brac, toys and clothing, including leather goods. Whatever you wanted – it was there. Traders would always be friendly and to my child's eye it felt like a magical land. I would wait with anticipation for Sunday to arrive as it was my dad's only day off and meant treats and delicious food at a Pakistani café called Sweet & Spicy. Sometimes he'd buy me a trinket; a musical jewellery box with a dancing ballerina, or a vintage handheld mirror. I'd try and remember favourite stalls, marking them in my head with a mental image so that we could visit them again the following week.

These weekly outings also meant peeking into a part of East London that was ever-changing, and introduced me to different foods and flavours. I would watch Dad select vegetables and fruits from stalls, chatting to the traders while checking for freshness. He'd point out unusual items to me, describing what they were and how you might cook them. We'd bump into his friends and the topic inevitably turned to food. Often these friends would be coming over for dinner that evening, so Dad would gather provisions for my mother to transform into feasts of fish and meat curries, vegetables and rice. We'd visit Taj Stores at 112 Brick Lane, a local institution and meeting point due to the simple fact it stocked Bangladeshi produce difficult to find elsewhere, including frozen fish and halal meat. When I was young the shop was half the size it is today and abuzz with people not only shopping but catching up with friends and exchanging news from home and abroad.

For many Bangladeshis living in London, Brick Lane is unofficially known as 'Banglatown'. In those days the market was a hub – a home away from home for British Bangladeshis. There was a strong Bangladeshi community that spanned from Aldgate and Whitechapel to Mile End, Limehouse and the Docklands – before the creation of Canary Wharf and the rise of Shoreditch as a pricy and desirable place to live and work. As with a lot of areas where gentrification is in full swing, people started being priced out of the area and many in the community moved towards outer East London and Essex.

Contemporary Brick Lane is still famed for the largest concentration of curry houses in London. Flanked by the East End on one side and the City on the other, a heady moment can transport you from small shops, eateries and street markets to slick skyscrapers and futuristic offices. This street is the artery that connects Shoreditch and Whitechapel, where the old East End and Bangladeshi London co-exist with a more current landscape of shops in cargo containers and ever-changing restaurants, bars and clubs. Street art is a permanent feature, where world-renowned artists leave their mark in celebration of the area and paint walls and bricks to life.

Step out of Whitechapel Underground Station and you'll be thrown deep into the sounds and smells of the Bangladeshi community, market traders calling out in Bengali to sell produce, with the odd Englishman doing the same, offering exotic vegetables to elderly Bangladeshi women who turn and chuckle at his broken Bengali. As you walk up to the Aldgate East

end of Brick Lane, you'll find plenty of places to eat cheaply and well: a plate piled high with delicious biriyani will cost you the princely sum of £5, in stark contrast to the Shoreditch end of the street where an (admittedly very tasty) Crosstown doughnut costs nearly the same. Just a stone's throw away there's Spitalfields, another old market area now fringed with ridiculously expensive property and designer shops.

Nothing reflects the changing demographic of this famous street more than the Brick Lane mosque. The building was first built as a church by Huguenots, Protestants who fled religious persecution in Catholic France during the 17th century. Around 50,000 sought refuge in England by sanction of Charles II and large numbers settled in Spitalfields and Brick Lane, bringing with them their exceptional weaving skills. These master weavers built on the existing silk industry in East London and flourished, catering to wealthy Londoners. Along Brick Lane, they built impressive townhouses for themselves and their employees as well as many churches, redefining the area. With the decline of the silk trade in the late 19th century, the French Huguenot community began to disperse, and a new wave of immigrants arrived from Russia.

Around 120,000 Ashkenazi Jews settled in England, escaping religious pogroms and economic hardship, and many of them chose the East End as their new home and started working in the textiles industry – or 'rag trade' as it came to be known. The church became a synagogue, those grand Huguenot townhouses were quickly split up into lodgings for workers, and again the area was transformed. As the Jewish community grew, the specialist bakeries and restaurants emerged that have become so iconic of the area. All that remains of many of them is their signage, but Beigel Shop and Beigel Bake, the two famous bagel shops on Brick Lane, are still going strong, as is Rinkoffs bakery in neighbouring Whitechapel.

By the time the synagogue became Brick Lane mosque in the mid 1970s, the area had already undergone another wave of immigration. While there had long been a history of seamen (or lascars) from what was then Bengal jumping ship and settling in the UK, the end of British rule in India in 1947 saw the arrival of many more Bengalis. Post Second World War, the UK was faced with a labour shortage, so immigration laws were relaxed to encourage people from the British colonies to come here to live and work. Then, in 1971, the country of Bangladesh was created out of a bloody civil war and as a result there was mass emigration to the UK. These new immigrants not only worked in the rag trade but increasingly in the growing Indian restaurant industry which was mainly owned and run by Bangladeshis from the Sylhet region. From the 1970s to the early 1990s, Dad used to work as a tailor in the leather garments industry just off Brick Lane and I remember the leather goods stalls and shops he'd take a keen interest in, comparing quality and workmanship. The trade declined in the 1990s, and Bashir & Sons is one the few remaining leather shops you'll see today, situated at 178 Brick Lane. All these people have left their legacies in modern-day Brick Lane and the Bengali or Bangladeshi dominance is now also shifting as newer communities from Somalia and Eastern Europe arrive and forge their own roots.

A decade or so ago, when I used to live in Bethnal Green – one of the entry points to this famous street – the disparity between the old-school curry houses on the south side (near Aldgate East Tube Station) and the trendy north side of Shoreditch used to be striking. Now there appears to be more of a natural flow. You'll find a growing number of cafés, bakeries and eateries nestled between the curry houses, hipster barbers, money change bureaus and fabric shops. Gradually, these lead onto vintage clothes stores and expensive boutiques. Art galleries housed in old Jewish shops with Yiddish signage echo the rich, multi-faceted past of the area. There's an antiques shop where my cousin and I read through old letters and postcards from people who lived in the area, telling stories from home and abroad: letters of love, friendship and the necessary telegram-like card from someone on holiday, announcing a birth or a visit. I love Brick Lane Bookshop at no. 166 – which used to be called Eastside Books when I was growing up.

Since moving out of the area my visits to Brick Lane were not as frequent as I'd have liked. Fast-forward to 2016 and there I was again, visiting almost every week – sometimes twice a week – for research and recipes and feeling just as much at home amongst the traders and markets as I used to as a child. I was on a mission to showcase the best and most delicious recipes from traders, restaurants and eateries that make up Brick Lane. In addition to my notebook and pen it was also imperative that I took along a healthy appetite to sample what was on offer.

This book is a celebration of what makes Brick Lane so special to me. Half of the recipes capture the home-cooking of the Bangladeshi community that has been living in the area for many years, as well as modern takes on Bangladeshi flavours. I've included some of my mother's recipes and techniques and some of

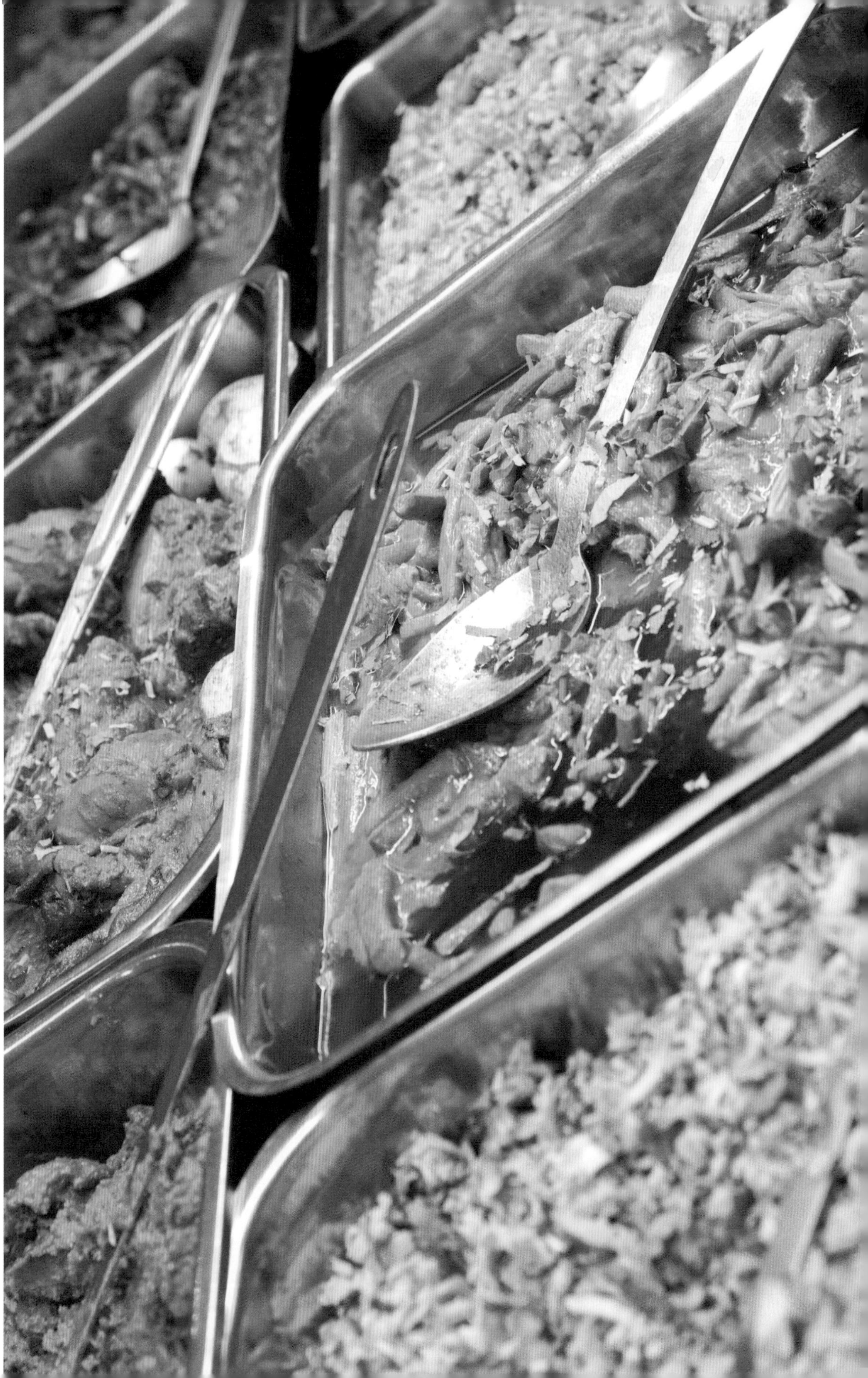

EVERY RECIPE I CAME ACROSS IS INTERWOVEN WITH A STORY AND I'D CHAT TO TRADERS ABOUT THEIR INSPIRATIONS AND THE FOOD THEY GREW UP EATING.

my own twists on classics. The rest are recipes generously contributed by street food traders, restaurants and eateries which showcase the range and diversity of cuisine that flows through the street, and reflect the incredibly global nature of Brick Lane.

During my visits I got to know and become friends with some of the most welcoming people living and working in the area. Every recipe I came across is interwoven with a story and I'd chat to traders about their inspirations and the food they grew up eating. The common thread amongst many of these businesses and traders is the need to bring a taste of home to London and to people of their diaspora, reflected in the particular way they prepare dishes, highlighting the best of their culinary cultures. On repeat visits I would notice that many of their customers were regulars who shared a sense of camaraderie that spanned beyond the minutes or hours they spent enjoying the food.

At Damascu Bite I spent a morning in the kitchen closely watching as the chef put together a traditional moussaka and tabbouleh and explained the best way to achieve authenticity, interspersed with stories of Syria and its food. I learnt that dishes made for weddings included mahallabi and was delighted to be given a recipe for it, which I've included in this book. Nadia at Chez Elles treated me to the best tarte aux amandes I've ever eaten, indulging my love of brown butter, while talking passionately about bringing authentic and affordable French cuisine to London – her adopted home. It was difficult to refuse the sweets Alauddin's owner produced while giving me a much anticipated tour of the kitchen where they make delicious Bangladeshi sweets, busy with giant karahis filled with syrup-infused sweets and frying oblongs of the famous kalojaam.

The Aldgate East end of Brick Lane houses several very authentic Bangladeshi cafés. What makes these cafés so unique is the amazing array of home-style dishes, displayed in deep steel platters. There's every kind of Bangladeshi fish and seafood – fried, curried and shredded into salads – as well as vegetable dishes and a smaller selection of meat. More unusual dishes include brain masala, a dish I tried with a little trepidation but found really delicious! It's sometimes fun to just pick whatever takes your fancy and let every delicious morsel surprise you. Dishes arrive all at once along with a plate of thinly sliced onions, green chillies, slices of lemon and a jug of water – much like mealtimes in Bangladeshi homes where sharing plates are customary. Bangladeshi sweet shops are dotted around these cafés, their windows full of traditional sweet and savoury snacks, trays piled high with shingara (Bengali spiced potato samosas) and colourful swirls of zilafi, or jalebi – a sweet popular all over the Indian subcontinent.

The market on Brick Lane that I loved so much as a child is now a collection of markets. The council-run market, which begins near Shoreditch and stretches to Buxton Street, includes stalls selling china, jewellery, bric-a-brac and clothes and is still very much like the market I remember from childhood. Traders are laid back and relaxed in comparison to their trendier counterparts further along the street. There is a street food section on the railway bridge after Cheshire Street where some contributors like St Sugar of London and The Big Bushi trade. Next there are the famous Truman Brewery-run markets. These include The Tea Rooms, which specialises in antiques, handmade items and baked goods, and the

wonderful Boiler House food hall, operating all weekend, with around 80 stalls. However, the largest space by far is the super-sized Sunday Upmarket which takes place in the Truman Brewery building on the corner of Brick Lane and Hanbury Street and includes around 140 food stalls such as Choco Fruit. Finally, a collection of permanent food trucks is situated at the back of the building, in an area called Ely's Yard.

The street food scene is organic, constantly adapting to the tastes and desires of the city. Whatever your heart (and stomach) desires, the market has you covered. There's Korean BBQ, Vietnamese banh-mi, Tibetan momos, and of course Indian chicken tikka and samosas. Meat lovers are spoilt for choice, with slow-cooked ribs, wings, burgers and smoked meats. Vegetarians and vegans are absolutely included in this tantalising food carnival, with Spanish-inspired vegan and vegetarian omelettes, paellas and favourites – veganised. If you have a sweet tooth you're in good hands. All kinds of cravings are catered for, from health-conscious energy bars to fragrant Turkish delight, brownies and doughnuts, oozing with chocolate and cream.

Sunday is undoubtedly the best time to visit the market, with around 80,000 people passing through. The street and the pockets in between come alive with people, food, and street performances. There are also occasional food and drink festivals which mostly take place in the Truman Brewery space. A multitude of independent eateries have appeared and claimed a piece of the Brick Lane cool – you'd never know the place was once considered a slum, more associated with crime and Jack the Ripper than artisan food. Sometimes while you're eating your bagel from one of the two authentic Jewish bagel shops – correctly spelt 'beigel' in the Ashkenazi manner – you'll spot groups of tourists on the market or Jack the Ripper tour, taking in the sights, smells and sounds of East London's most enduring foodie hub.

I'd like to say a special thank you to the traders and restaurants who have welcomed me into their kitchens and stalls and have shared favourite recipes not only from their menus but also from their families. Their warmth and kindness made collating and writing their recipes such a joy. I've carefully curated over 90 recipes to take you from breakfast to dinner and everything in between. There are personal childhood favourites and recipes which celebrate the multi-layering of flavours, such my chai malai cake, a favourite amongst friends and family that is inspired by Asian sweets and spiced tea. I've included delicious recipes from street traders such as The Big Bushi's sushi burritos and The Patate's beef bourguignon burgers, as well as restaurant favourites such as Enoteca Pomaio's Italian tomato and ricotta crochettes. There's a recipe for my pineapple and Naga chilli chicken, which blends the Bangladeshi flavours of Brick Lane with London tastes.

Writing this book has been a labour of love. It meant taking a closer look at the food culture of an ever-changing part of London, famous the world over. Despite undergoing many changes, the heart of Brick Lane is still large and generous, welcoming those who love to eat into its fold. Whatever your cravings, I hope you'll love cooking recipes from this book as much as I've enjoyed sharing them with you.

WHATEVER YOUR HEART (AND STOMACH) DESIRES, THE MARKET HAS YOU COVERED.

KITCHEN ESSENTIALS

A GOOD, SHARP KNIFE —————— Do not underestimate the importance of this. It will make your life so much easier when it comes to chopping and slicing, especially for parties (translation – more chopping and slicing). And do invest in a knife sharpener if possible.

WHISK —————— A solid whisk is always a good investment if you don't have one already.

ELECTRIC WHISK —————— Not absolutely essential but cuts down a lot on the elbow grease and time required to whip cream, frostings and egg whites.

WOK —————— Either an oriental wok, an Indian karahi, or a deep frying pan.

SMALL TO MEDIUM SIZED PANS —————— Standard set of cooking pans, usually a trio.

HEAVY-BOTTOMED PAN —————— Useful for making slow-cooked dishes.

SKILLET OR GRIDDLE PAN —————— Without the ridges.

PESTLE AND MORTAR —————— Another essential item, regardless of type of cuisine. Great for making pastes and crushing garlic and ginger.

BLENDER/SMOOTHIE MAKER —————— Great for making pastes, juices, shakes and of course, smoothies!

SET OF MEASURING SPOONS —————— Not all teaspoons and tablespoons are created equal, so do invest in these. Look for a set that goes from 1 tablespoon to $\frac{1}{8}$ teaspoon.

WEIGHING SCALES —————— Useful for any kitchen and a must for baking.

A NOTE ON
INGREDIENTS

PANCH PHORON —————— This classic five spice blend is essential to Bengali cooking and has the most amazing aroma. Made up of nigella, mustard, fenugreek, cumin and fennel seeds, it is usually used at the start of cooking a dish as the seeds pop and quickly release their flavours in hot oil after a couple of seconds. Alternatively, you can use it when you are making a tarka or tempering a dhal for added aroma towards the end of cooking. Panch phoron is also great added to chutneys and pickles for a bold and unusual flavour.

GRAM FLOUR (OR BESAN) —————— Or, chickpea flour. This flour is a great gluten free flour often used in batters for pakoras, fritters and Indian sweets. It can also be substituted for wheat flour in baking – especially suited to spiced cakes, as the flavour can be quite intense if it's not fried or toasted first.

CHAAT MASALA —————— This popular spice blend is used in savoury street food dishes across the Indian subcontinent. The blend typically includes black salt, pepper, dried mango powder, cumin, coriander, dried ginger and asafoetida. It's pungent, a little smoky and salty, and really packs a punch in terms of flavour. Use in spice mixes and sauces, or sprinkle onto creamy dips for a spicy note.

GROUND CARDAMOM
(FROM GREEN CARDAMOM PODS) —————— Cardamom is the second most expensive spice in the world after saffron, and so versatile. It's difficult to find ready-ground cardamom and I'd steer clear of it even if you do find some as the flavour and fragrance weakens if stored for too long. For that sweet and earthy burst of cardamom, always grind your own when you need it by extracting the seeds from the pods and grinding them in a coffee mill or mortar and pestle. The darker the seeds, the better the flavour will be, so only select the black or very dark brown ones, especially if you're making sweets.

JAGGERY — I absolutely love to use jaggery in cooking. This fudgy unrefined sugar, also referred to as *gur,* is made from palm sap and is sold in solid blocks or rounds. It is used for both sweet and savoury dishes and is a staple ingredient in curries, broths and marinades, as well as being crucial to Bengali desserts such as rice pudding. Jaggery is widely available in the world food section of larger supermarkets; however if you pop in to your local Asian grocery store you will find a much larger range, varying in colour and texture. I'd stick to a deep golden one as it has the most versatile flavour. Once you open a packet remember to store in a cool dry place.

GHEE — Otherwise known as clarified butter, ghee is butter with the milk solids removed so that you are left with a clear fat. It's the fat of choice in most South Asian households and imparts the most delicious nutty flavour and aroma. Ghee has become a trendy health food in recent years, although it's been widely used for its Ayurvedic (holistic healing) benefits in the Indian subcontinent for over 3,000 years. It is used mainly in meat and chicken dishes and in South Indian and Middle Eastern sweet-making, particularly Indian laddoos and barfis and Syrian kunafa. If you're familiar with beurre noisette or browned butter then you'll know it's similar in aroma. To ensure your ghee doesn't go off, store in the fridge once opened and it will keep well for several months.

RAPESEED OIL — I use this oil a lot in my cooking as it has a high smoking point – so it's perfect for frying and a good alternative to dairy in cakes. Rapeseed oil is also healthier than vegetable or sunflower oil as it is high in omega-3 and very low in saturated fats. The flavour is neutral so a good option for delicate fish dishes and baking. I tend to fry savoury and sweet things in it, as you're not left with that fatty oil residue once your food has been cooked.

AGAVE SYRUP/NECTAR — This amber-coloured sweetener is produced from the sap of the Mexican agave plant and is sweeter and less viscous than honey, so a little goes a long way. It has a high fructose content and is great in syrups, smoothies and baking as an alternative to sugar.

CACAO POWDER ——————— Sometimes sold as raw cocoa, cacao powder is cold-pressed from un-roasted, raw cocoa beans. Said to be a superfood with many health benefits, the flavour is quite earthy and a little bitter. Use it the same way you'd use cocoa powder. It's available to buy in larger supermarkets or health food stores.

DRIED ROSE PETALS ——————— Use ready-torn petals to scatter over cakes and puddings, or for a fresher look and more vibrant colour, buy whole dried rosebuds and pull them apart. I also use them in a Middle Eastern inspired spice mix, or grind and add to sugar for a pretty-looking 'dust' over biscuits and cakes.

ROSEWATER ——————— The rosewater I use in recipes in this book is the Asian variety which is less intense than rose extract or essence. Look for brands such as TRS or East End which are readily available in most major supermarkets as well as your local Asian grocery store.

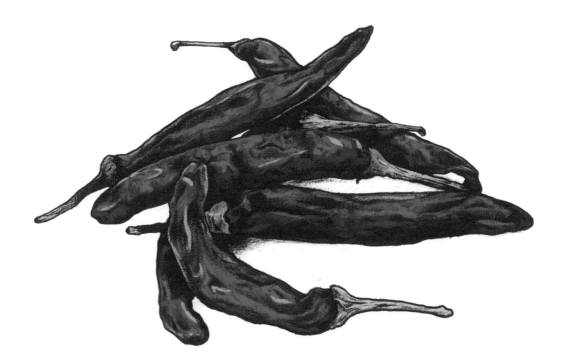

Most ingredients in the book are easily available in the UK, often in larger supermarkets and Asian grocers. If you're in London, a few steps away from Brick Lane you'll find a few of the usual supermarkets and smaller independent stores. But you can't beat Taj Stores (112 Brick Lane, www.tajstores.co.uk) for wide selection and all-round shopping experience. This Bangladeshi supermarket is a local institution and first opened its doors in 1936. Along with catering to the eclectic taste of London, the store sells fresh meat, frozen seafood and a wonderful array of fruits and vegetables. There's an exciting mix of the familiar with the unfamiliar on display and the store remains firmly attuned to the changing needs of its client base. I've managed to pick up dried rose petals, dragon fruit, lychee and mastic (gum arabic) as well as Middle Eastern seasonings. You can even get hold of some kitchen/serve ware if you're pressed for time – it really is a one stop shop. For South East Asian recipes it's always worth popping to Chinatown for a browse for things like black fermented soybeans.

If your local stores don't stock any of the more obscure items, try Sous Chef (online only: www.souschef.co.uk) which has pretty much everything you'll need, including pistachio paste and black garlic. The Red Rickshaw is another great online store which stocks a huge selection of Asian grocery items and spices. Their website is www.redrickshaw.com.

SPECIAL DIETARY REQUIREMENTS

ALL THE RECIPES ARE FLAGGED WITH THE FOLLOWING
SYMBOLS TO MAKE IT EASIER FOR PEOPLE WITH SPECIAL
DIETARY REQUIREMENTS TO USE. YOU CAN ALSO TWEAK
A LOT OF THE RECIPES TO MAKE THEM SUITABLE FOR
RESTRICTED DIETS – CHECK THE RECIPES
FOR SUGGESTIONS.

V ——————————— VEGAN
GF —————————— GLUTEN FREE
WF —————————— WHEAT FREE
EF —————————— EGG FREE
DF —————————— DAIRY FREE

MOVE ON UP
SMOOTHIE BOWL

STAY TROPICAL
BOILER HOUSE
FOOD HALL

Serves 2
WF, GF, EF

Smoothie bowls make a great breakfast dish that also looks impressive. Thick and filling, this smoothie was created by Jamie at the Stay Tropical stall to provide the kind of kick you might need for a Sunday morning hangover cure and to fuel your day of shopping at Brick Lane. This recipe is jam-packed with nutrients, antioxidants, carbs and a generous dose of chia seeds. It tastes incredible and will make you feel incredible when you think of all that goodness.

1 avocado, peeled and de-stoned

200g chia seeds

2 handfuls of fresh spinach

1 frozen mango

6 tablespoons natural
    fat-free yogurt

600ml almond milk

2 Medjool dates

2 teaspoons cacao powder

¼ teaspoon pink Himalayan
    sea salt

2 bananas

2 tablespoons agave syrup

handful of raspberries

10 strawberries

2 kiwis

4 tablespoons blueberries

4 tablespoons granola

Throw everything except the strawberries, kiwis, blueberries and granola in a blender and blitz until smooth. Hull and slice the strawberries and set aside. Top and tail the kiwis, (peel them if you like) then chop into thick slices.

Once your smoothie is ready pour into two bowls and top with the kiwi and strawberry slices. Sprinkle over the blueberries and granola (here's when you can make your smoothie bowl Instagram-ready and arrange everything decoratively) and serve.

BUTTERMILK
PANCAKES

Serves 4

Pancakes are one of my favourite things to eat on a lazy Sunday morning and you can find them on the menu at many of the Brick Lane eateries and food stalls. But sometimes you just want to stay in and this recipe is so fool-proof you have no excuses not to make them at home. These pancakes are light, fluffy and not overly sweet, so you can add a variety of sweet or savoury toppings. I love them with some golden syrup and whipped cream, which is simple and satisfying. However, for a real treat, pair them with my rhubarb, rose and cardamom compote (page 28), add a dollop of Greek yoghurt and scatter with some toasted, flaked almonds – plus some organic honey if you like yours extra sweet!

2 medium eggs

6 tablespoons caster sugar

150ml milk

150ml buttermilk

1 teaspoon vanilla extract

1 tablespoon melted butter

200g self-raising flour

⅛ teaspoon salt

½ teaspoon baking powder

¼ teaspoon bicarbonate of soda

rapeseed oil, for cooking

In a mixing bowl beat together the eggs and sugar with a whisk, then add the milk, buttermilk, vanilla and melted butter. Add 100g of the flour, salt, baking powder and bicarbonate of soda and mix well. Mix in the remaining flour and whisk until you have a thick, pourable batter.

Heat a griddle or wide frying pan on medium-low heat and brush with a teaspoon of oil. When it's hot, pour in a small ladleful of batter and gently swirl the pan to make a pancake about 12cm in diameter. You should be able to make two to three pancakes at a time, depending on the size of your pan.

Cook for about a minute until bubbles begin to appear on the surface, then flip over and cook for another minute until golden around the edges. If they seem to brown too quickly just turn the heat down a bit for the next batch.

Re-grease the pan as needed (usually after two batches) and repeat until you use up all the batter. You should end up with 12 to 16 pancakes. Serve in a stack with your favourite syrup or fruit compote and cream.

Cook's tip – if you can't get hold of buttermilk, try making your own. Just stir a teaspoon of cider vinegar into 150ml of milk, let it sit for five minutes and voilà!

RHUBARB, ROSE & CARDAMOM COMPOTE

Serves 4-6
V, WF, GF

Inspired by Asian and Middle Eastern flavours, this compote has subtle floral notes of rosewater and fragrant cardamom, which perfectly complement sweet and tart British rhubarb. It's definitely a seasonal recipe, so grab some gorgeous pink stems of rhubarb when you see them appear at your favourite fruit and veg store. Forced rhubarb is available out of season but I prefer to use field or allotment grown, which is available from spring until early autumn and has a better colour and flavour. I didn't eat rhubarb much until my dad started growing it several years ago, and now I look forward to it every year. I am absolutely biased when it comes to cardamom: I love it and tend to favour it in sweet dishes so I was glad to discover that rhubarb is made for this spice.

500g rhubarb, cut into
  2cm pieces
juice of ½ lemon
300g granulated sugar
½ teaspoon ground cardamom
2 tablespoons rosewater

Put the rhubarb, lemon juice and sugar in a heavy-bottomed pan and stir together. Let it sit for 15 minutes as this gives the sugar time to draw out water from the rhubarb. Add the cardamom and bring to a boil on medium-high heat, stirring occasionally, until the sugar is dissolved – three to four minutes. Reduce the heat to medium, add the rosewater and simmer for about eight minutes, until the rhubarb starts to break up and the mixture has thickened.

Cool completely before serving over pancakes, yoghurt or ice cream. It's also delicious as a filling for cakes with buttercream or fresh cream. The compote keeps well in the fridge for up to two weeks. Just pour into a clean container or jar with a tight-fitting lid.

SPICY OMELETTE

Serves 4
WF, GF, DF

Weekends mean time for relaxation and fun and of course a leisurely breakfast after a busy week. A stroll through the market with friends and family is what I've grown up doing on my Sundays, and this omelette is a family favourite. There's a bit of heat, some sweetness from the onions and lots of herby goodness from the fresh coriander. And the best thing is you only need to cook one big omelette to share between four people. Just toast a stack of bread and add your favourite condiments for a lovely brunch to start your day.

4 large eggs
1 teaspoon salt
1 medium onion, finely sliced
1 tomato, chopped
2 green chillies, finely chopped
½ red pepper, chopped
½ teaspoon cayenne pepper
½ teaspoon ground cumin
¼ teaspoon ground turmeric
3 tablespoons fresh coriander, chopped
2 tablespoons oil
crushed black pepper, to taste

Whisk the eggs in a bowl and season with the salt and some black pepper, then add the onion, tomato, chillies, red pepper, cayenne, cumin, turmeric and chopped coriander. Mix everything well.

Heat the oil in a large non-stick frying pan over medium-low heat. Pour the omelette mixture into the pan, swirling the pan a little so that the mixture is distributed evenly. Cover and cook for three to four minutes, until golden on the underside. Using a large spatula carefully flip the omelette over and cook uncovered for a further two minutes or so, then cut into quarters and serve.

KIMCHIJEON
KIMCHI PANCAKES

SSAMBOP
BOILER HOUSE FOOD
HALL

Serves 2
V
‒

Koreans are crazy for kimchi – a salted and fermented vegetable side dish with a pungent, spicy taste. This love of kimchi has spread across the UK into homes, restaurants and food stalls and it is one of the dishes that Kisu of Ssambop loves to eat. When I spoke to him on a visit to Brick Lane about vegetarian dishes, he recommended something with cabbage kimchi, and later sent me this delicious, easy recipe.

150g cabbage kimchi, chopped
½ small onion, chopped
½ teaspoon salt
½ teaspoon sugar
75g flour

vegetable oil, to cook

Place the kimchi, onion, salt, sugar and flour into a bowl. Add 50ml water and mix well. The batter should be fairly thick but still runny enough to pour – similar to regular pancake batter.

Heat a frying pan over medium heat and add a teaspoon of oil. Move the pan around so it's evenly coated. When the oil is hot pour in a small ladleful of batter and cook for a minute or so, until the edges are brown and small bubbles appear on the surface. Flip over and cook for another minute until both sides are crispy and slightly browned.

Repeat with the remaining batter, re-greasing the pan as necessary – you should end up with about six pancakes. Slice into pieces and serve.

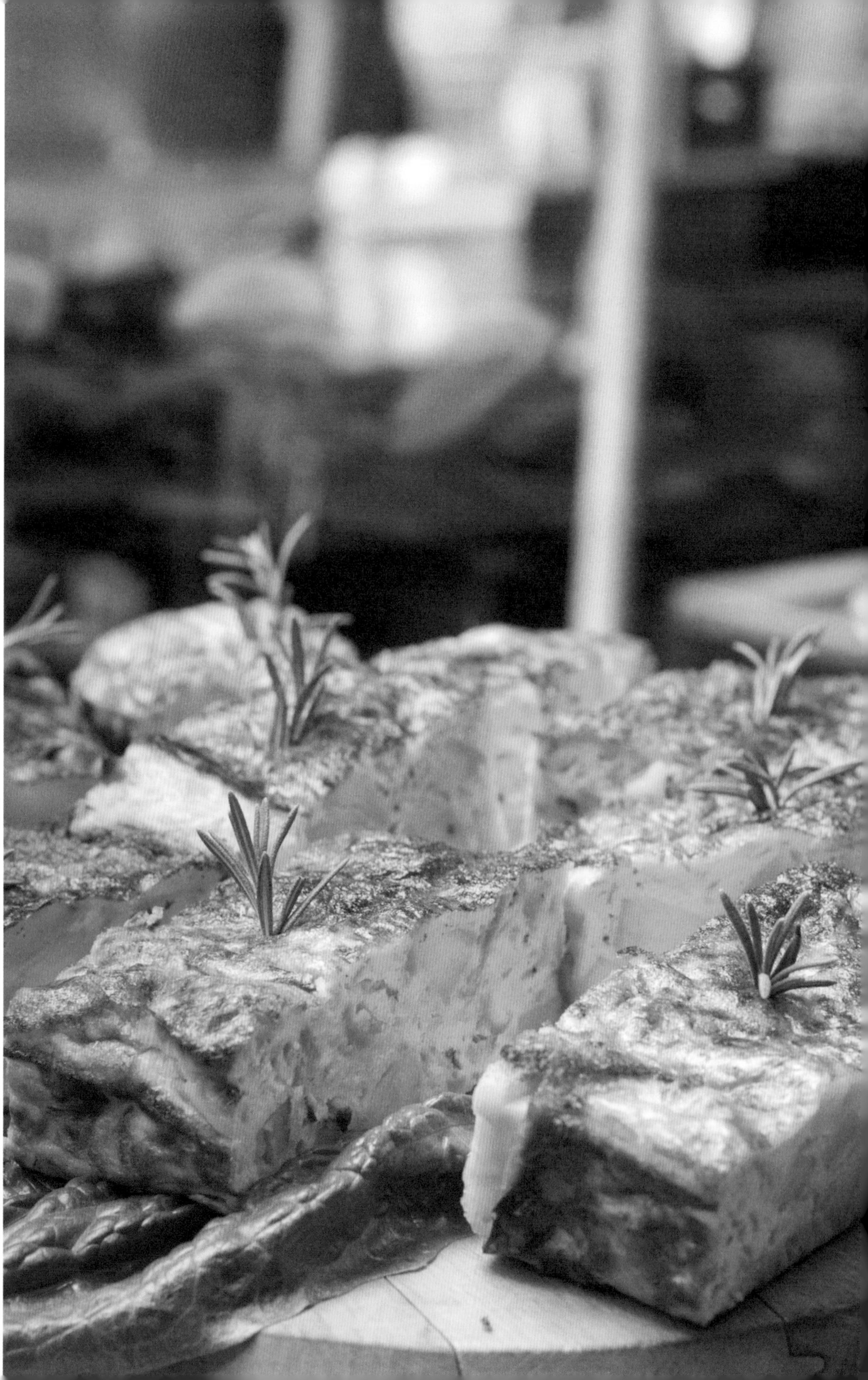

TORTILLA

Tortilla is an easy Mediterranean favourite and a popular dish on the Café 1001 menu. This baked version of the classic Spanish potato omelette is flavoured with rosemary and gently caramelised sweet onions and I love it. Make sure to cool your potatoes before adding to the egg mix; otherwise you'll end up with scrambled eggs.

2 tablespoons olive oil

2 medium onions, finely sliced

1 bay leaf

500g cypress potatoes, peeled and cut into 2cm chunks

1 teaspoon salt

6 large eggs

1 tablespoon fresh rosemary, finely chopped

½ teaspoon black pepper

500ml vegetable oil, to deep fry

First make your sweet onions. Pour the olive oil in a frying pan over low heat. Add the sliced onion and bay leaf and cook for 40 to 45 minutes, stirring occasionally, until the onions have reduced and are completely soft and lightly browned. You'll end up with about four heaped tablespoons of sweet, caramelised onions. Set aside to cool.

Throw the potatoes into a bowl and mix with the salt. Set aside for ten minutes. Heat the vegetable oil in a deep pan over a high heat (140°C) – test it's hot enough by dropping in a piece of potato which should start sizzling immediately. Deep fry the potatoes for 12 minutes or until golden and tender, then drain and leave to cool for at least 15 minutes. At this point preheat your oven to 180°C (160°C fan).

Whisk the eggs in a mixing bowl and add the cooled sweet onion mixture, rosemary and black pepper. Throw in the fried potato pieces and mix well. Line a deep baking dish and pour in the mixture.

Bake for 25 to 30 minutes, or until the tortilla is golden brown on top and cooked in the middle. Test it's done by inserting a small knife or skewer in the centre – if it comes out clean your tortilla is ready. Cool for ten minutes before serving.

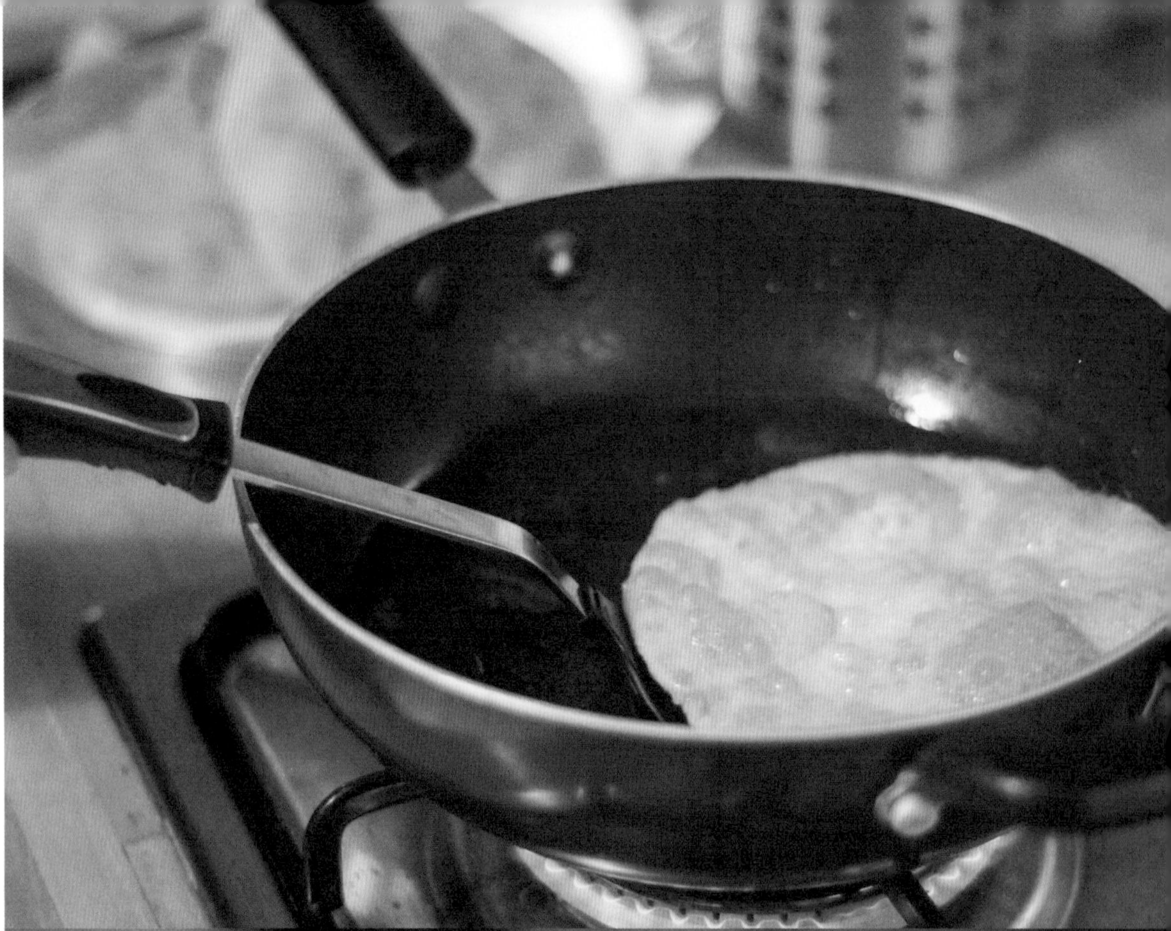

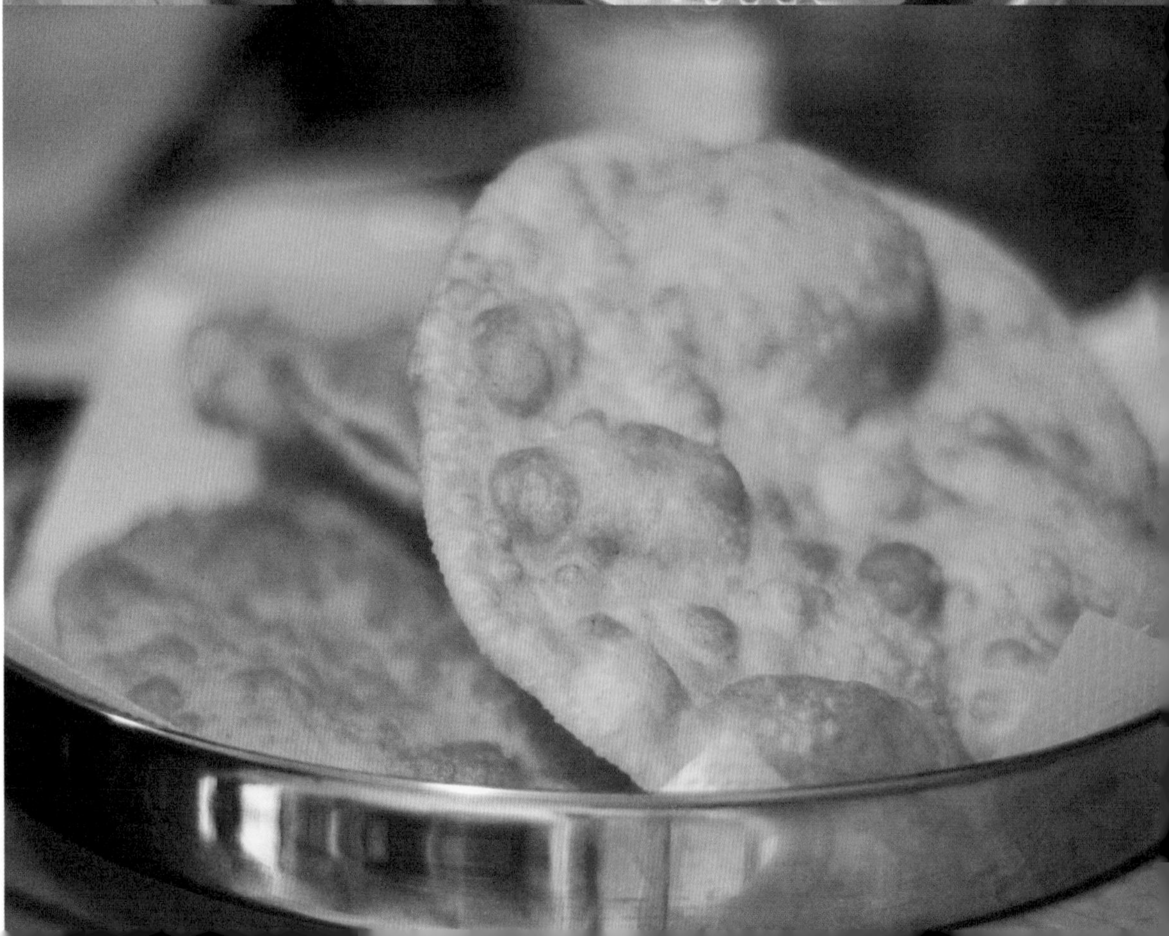

PURI
FRIED FLATBREAD

Serves 4-6
V
—

Bangladeshi Brick Lane brunch inspiration includes these wonderful crispy, fried flatbreads called puri, which are usually accompanied by lightly spiced potato or aloo bhaji. You can also serve them with a dish of shemai or sweet vermicelli pudding (page 41) which is equally delicious as the fried bread is perfect for scooping up the sugary, thick pudding. Try it both ways and brunch like a Bengali.

250g plain flour, plus more
  for dusting
½ teaspoon salt
2 tablespoons rapeseed oil

500ml vegetable oil, to deep fry

Put the flour into a mixing bowl with the salt and rapeseed oil. Add 140ml water and knead to form a soft dough. If the dough seems too dry add another tablespoon of water. Cover with a cloth and let it rest for 20 minutes. Knead the dough for a few minutes and then divide into 12 equal portions.

Dust a surface with flour and roll out into thin rounds, approximately 12cm in diameter.

Heat the vegetable oil in a deep pan on high heat. Once hot, carefully slide the first puri into the hot oil. It will sink to the bottom and then rise, puffing up. Once this happens carefully turn it over, checking it's golden underneath, and cook the other side for another 30 seconds or so. Once the puri is golden on both sides remove with a slotted spoon, and drain on kitchen paper. Repeat with the remaining dough and serve piping hot.

ALOO BHAJI
SPICED POTATOES

Serves 4-6
V, WF, GF

Aloo bhaji and freshly fried puri is a classic breakfast combination. The potatoes are spicy without being hot, so they make a perfect brunch, followed by steaming cups of spiced tea. This dish is really versatile and you'll often find it in the unassuming Bangladeshi cafés of Brick Lane, as it's a staple in the Bangladeshi community no matter the time of day.

3 tablespoons oil
½ teaspoon cumin seeds
1 teaspoon mustard seeds
1 medium onion, finely sliced
1½ teaspoons salt
½ teaspoon ground turmeric
½ teaspoon ground cumin
½ teaspoon chilli powder
3 medium potatoes, peeled
  and cut into small cubes
1 green chilli, chopped
1–2 tablespoons fresh coriander,
  chopped

Heat the oil in a frying pan over medium-high heat. Add the cumin and mustard seeds. Once the mustard seeds begin to pop (about 30 seconds) add the sliced onion and salt.

Sauté for a couple of minutes until the onions are translucent and then add the ground turmeric, cumin and chilli powder. Cook for another minute and then stir in the potatoes and green chilli. Add 50ml of water, bring to a gentle simmer and then reduce the heat to medium-low.

Cover and cook for five minutes, then stir and add the chopped coriander. Cook for a further three or four minutes (still covered) until the potatoes are soft but still hold their shape. This dish is always served with freshly fried puri (see page 37).

SHEMAI
SWEET VERMICELLI PUDDING

Serves 6
EF

A sweet, milky pudding fragrant with spices and synonymous with breakfast in Bengali homes. The recipe calls for a soft, airy type of vermicelli called Lachcha Semai. The Pran variety is the best type to use and is available in Bangladeshi shops; however you can easily substitute this for the same amount of Pakistani or Indian vermicelli which is readily available in Asian stores. Just make sure to cook the vermicelli for an extra five minutes in the milk and adjust the sugar to your taste. You can use butter instead of ghee, but keep in mind it won't give you that delicious nutty flavour.

1 litre whole milk
120g sugar
1 stick cinnamon
1 bay leaf
6 cardamom pods
1 tablespoon ghee
200g Pran Lachcha
  Semai vermicelli
1 tablespoon roughly chopped
  pistachios or almonds

In a pan heat the milk, sugar, cinnamon, bay leaf and cardamom. Gently simmer on medium-low heat for five minutes so that the spices infuse the milk. Keep an eye on the pan and stir occasionally to stop the milk burning or boiling over.

Heat the ghee in a frying pan on medium heat, then add the vermicelli and fry for a minute until very lightly golden. Add the toasted vermicelli to the spiced milk and cook for four to five minutes on medium-high until the milk has been almost completely absorbed and you are left with a moderately thick, custard-like consistency.

Serve the shemai hot or cold, garnished with chopped nuts. If you want to re-heat it, just add a dash of milk to lighten it a little and warm through on the stove over low heat.

SPICED DATE, CARROT
& COCONUT LOAF

Serves 10
DF

I believe sweet things are essential for weekend indulgence, and to fuel a day wandering around the market. This loaf is delicious eaten warm and cut into chunky slices. What makes it so special is the combination of sweet carrots, sticky dates and coconut mixed in with warming spices that make you feel all cosy inside. Set yourself up for the day with a slice topped with a dollop of Greek yoghurt and a sprinkling of almonds.

200g soft pitted dates
2 medium carrots, grated
½ teaspoon salt
100g granulated sugar
2 medium eggs
1 teaspoon mixed spice
½ teaspoon ground cinnamon
1 teaspoon vanilla extract
80ml rapeseed oil
150g self-raising flour
75g desiccated coconut

23cm x 13cm loaf tin

Preheat the oven to 190°C (170°C fan). Grease and line your loaf tin.

Place the dates in a bowl with two tablespoons of water and then blitz with a hand blender until you have a smooth purée. Set aside.

Put the grated carrot in a bowl and mix thoroughly with salt and sugar – this softens the carrots and gives a more even bake. Mix in the eggs, mixed spice, cinnamon, vanilla and oil and then slowly incorporate the flour. Add the puréed dates and desiccated coconut and mix well to form a smooth batter.

Pour into your loaf tin and bake for 50 to 60 minutes, or until the loaf is golden on top and a skewer poked into the middle comes out clean. Cool in the tin for at least half an hour before slicing.

VEGAN, GLUTEN FREE, NUT FREE PUMPKIN LOAF

ST SUGAR
OF LONDON
STREET FOOD
MARKET

Serves 10
V, GF, WF

As the description suggests, this loaf is a free-from delight, brought to you by Enzo and his wife Sona of St Sugar of London. St Sugar's story began in 2009 when they started trading in Brick Lane. Passionate about healthy living and baking, they create delicious artisan baked goods with an emphasis on free-from and specialist baking that keeps up with changing food trends and lifestyles. Paleo, ketogenic and vegan palates are all catered for. Packed full of natural, unrefined ingredients and healthy fats, this is a feel-good kind of recipe, which means you can have your cake and eat it too!

---

1 small pumpkin

120g chickpea flour

100g cornflour

220g dark brown sugar

65g caster sugar

125ml olive oil

75ml coconut milk

1 teaspoon bicarbonate of soda

½ teaspoon salt

½ teaspoon ground nutmeg

¾ teaspoon ground cinnamon

25g desiccated coconut

23cm x 13cm loaf tin

Preheat your oven to 200°C (180°C fan). Grease and line your loaf tin.

First make the pumpkin purée. Quarter the pumpkin and place on a baking sheet. Roast in the oven for 60 to 90 minutes, or until fork-tender – if the pumpkin starts to brown too much just cover loosely with a piece of foil. When the pumpkin is soft, discard the seeds and scoop out the pulp. Reduce the oven temperature to 180°C (160°C fan). Either roughly mash the pumpkin pulp or, for a smoother consistency, purée it in a blender. Sift the chickpea flour and cornflour into a mixing bowl and combine with the dark brown sugar, caster sugar, oil, coconut milk, bicarbonate of soda, salt, nutmeg and cinnamon. Beat in 250g of the pumpkin pulp, add the coconut and pour the batter into the prepared tin.

Bake for 60 to 75 minutes and then cool completely on a wire rack before serving.

RICE FLOUR & CINNAMON DOUGHNUTS

Serves 4-6
V

These doughnuts are loosely based on a Bangladeshi fried cake recipe called *handesh* or *teler pitha,* traditionally made for special occasions. I don't think I've ever seen them on a menu here in the UK, but they are intrinsic to Bangladeshi food culture. I've simplified the recipe for a basic sugar handesh and added my own little twist of cinnamon. It is so easy – I don't use scales to weigh out the ingredients, but just measure out a ramekin each of the flours, then add another two thirds of a ramekin of sugar – alternatively, you could use a small teacup. The rice flour helps to create crunch, and the sugar caramelises while frying, making the doughnuts extra crispy. Make sure to coat them in the powdered sugar and cinnamon mix while they're still hot for a super flavoursome exterior.

FOR THE DOUGHNUTS:

1 ramekin plain flour

1 ramekin rice flour

⅔ ramekin caster sugar

500ml rapeseed oil, to deep fry

FOR THE DUSTING:

6 tablespoons icing sugar

1½ teaspoons ground cinnamon

Put the flours into a mixing bowl with the sugar. Start with one and a half ramekins of water and add it slowly, whisking everything together until you have a smooth and thick batter. The batter should fall easily if you drop some from a spoon. If the batter is too thick just add a little more water. Leave it to rest 15 to 20 minutes to help soften the rice flour.

Place the icing sugar and cinnamon into a large, clean, dry bowl and mix together with a whisk. Set aside.

Heat the oil in a wok or deep frying pan over medium-high heat. Give the batter a stir and then use a small ladle or a largish spoon to drop the mixture into the oil – each one should be a bit more than a tablespoon. You can probably fit in about six at a time.

Fry the doughnuts for four to five minutes, or until they are golden brown all over, turning them over a couple of times. Remove from the oil with a slotted spoon and drain on a tray lined with kitchen paper.

When you've fried all the doughnuts, transfer them from the kitchen paper to the bowl with the powdered sugar and cinnamon and toss around until all the doughnuts are coated. Serve warm.

CHESS
FUN
FREE

SNACKS
SMALL
PLATES
SNACKS

CHANACHUR
BOMBAY MIX WITH ONIONS, CHILLIES & LEMON

Serves 6
V

Boishaki Mela is a festival which welcomes the Bengali New Year, and it weaves through Brick Lane every year with elaborate processions, music and dance. There's something magical about public celebrations where everyone is welcome to join in. Street food stalls are an essential part of Boishaki and there's always a long line of festival-goers queuing up for chanachur – one of my favourite snacks growing up. It's very moreish: the crispy Bombay mix pastry softens a little in lemon juice, while sharp, thinly sliced onions and finely chopped green chillies add freshness and crunch. An occasional burst of pomegranate sweetness is one of my favourite personal additions. This is especially good during hot summer days, served with a cold drink.

275g regular Bombay mix
  (make sure it's not an
  extra hot kind)
1 medium red onion,
  finely chopped
2 green chillies, finely chopped
2 red chillies, finely chopped
4 tablespoons fresh coriander,
  chopped
juice of 1 lemon
3-4 tablespoons fresh
  pomegranate seeds

Simply pour the Bombay mix into a container with a lid and add the onion, chillies, coriander and lemon juice. Place the lid back on the container and shake vigorously for several seconds. Open the lid and stir through the pomegranate seeds just before serving.

Cook's tip – make sure to mix everything together just before serving; otherwise your Bombay mix will become soggy.

CHILLI CHEESE
SAMOSAS

Makes 16
EF

Samosas can be found in virtually all the Indian (or rather, Bangladeshi) curry houses along Brick Lane. You'll even find them on some Indian food stalls on market days. The triangular parcels are usually filled with a spiced potato mixture or lamb mince, but I make mine with a slightly different filling, which reminds me of one of my favourite English snacks, cheese and onions pasties. I use a mixture of Indian paneer and English cheddar with heat from chopped green chillies and some bite from finely sliced onions. The pastry is light and flaky, despite being fried. It's a hybrid snack: part samosa, part pasty, and ridiculously tasty.

FOR THE FILLING:

2 tablespoons rapeseed oil

1 small onion, finely chopped

⅔ teaspoon salt

3-4 green chillies,
  finely chopped

1 teaspoon cumin

½ teaspoon paprika

½ teaspoon garam masala

175g paneer, grated

175g medium cheddar, grated

Make the filling first. Heat the oil in a frying pan over medium heat, then add the onions, salt and chillies and sauté for a few minutes until the onions are translucent. Add the cumin, paprika and garam masala and cook for another minute, and then turn off the heat. Tip the paneer into the hot pan and stir through quickly (you don't want the paneer to melt), then put the mixture into a bowl and leave to cool for a couple of minutes. Mix in the cheddar until well combined. Check the seasoning and adjust if needed, and then cool completely – about 45 minutes.

While the filling is cooling prepare your pastry. Put the flour, salt and oil into a bowl and rub together with your fingertips until you have fine crumbs. Add 100ml of lukewarm water to form a firm dough. Cover and rest for at least 20 minutes.

FOR THE PASTRY:

250g plain flour, plus more
   for dusting
½ teaspoon salt
4 tablespoons oil

500ml rapeseed oil, to deep fry

When you are ready to assemble your samosas, tip the dough onto a lightly floured surface and knead for a few minutes. This will help release the gluten in the dough and ensure a flaky, yet firm crust which will hold its shape once fried. Divide the dough into eight portions and roll each one into a thin circle around 15cm in diameter. Cut each circle in half to give you 16 half-moon shapes, and rotate them so the curved edge is closest to you.

Place a heaped tablespoon of filling at the centre of a piece of pastry, leaving about 1cm space top and bottom. Brush the edges with water, and then fold the left side over the filling in the centre. Press down the pastry along the bottom seam, and then fold the right side down to form a triangle with a curved bottom edge. Pinch all the edges and the point of the triangle together so the filling is completely sealed in. Repeat for the remaining samosas.

Heat the oil in a deep pan over high heat. You can check if the oil is hot enough by dropping a small piece of bread into the oil. If it rises easily to the surface your oil is ready. Drop a few samosas at a time into the oil and then reduce the heat to low.

Fry the samosas for around four minutes, turning in the oil to ensure an even, golden colour. Remove with a slotted spoon and drain on kitchen paper. Before you fry the next batch, raise the heat back up to high to bring the oil back up to temperature and reduce to low once the samosas are in. Serve hot with your favourite chutney: I like to eat these with English red onion chutney for a little sweetness that also works well with the cheese.

Cook's tip – if for some reason you don't eat the samosas straight away, cool them completely, uncovered, and then place in an airtight container. This helps them stay a little flaky until the next day – when they can either be eaten cold (great for picnics!) or warmed up for around six minutes in a preheated oven at 190°C (170°C fan).

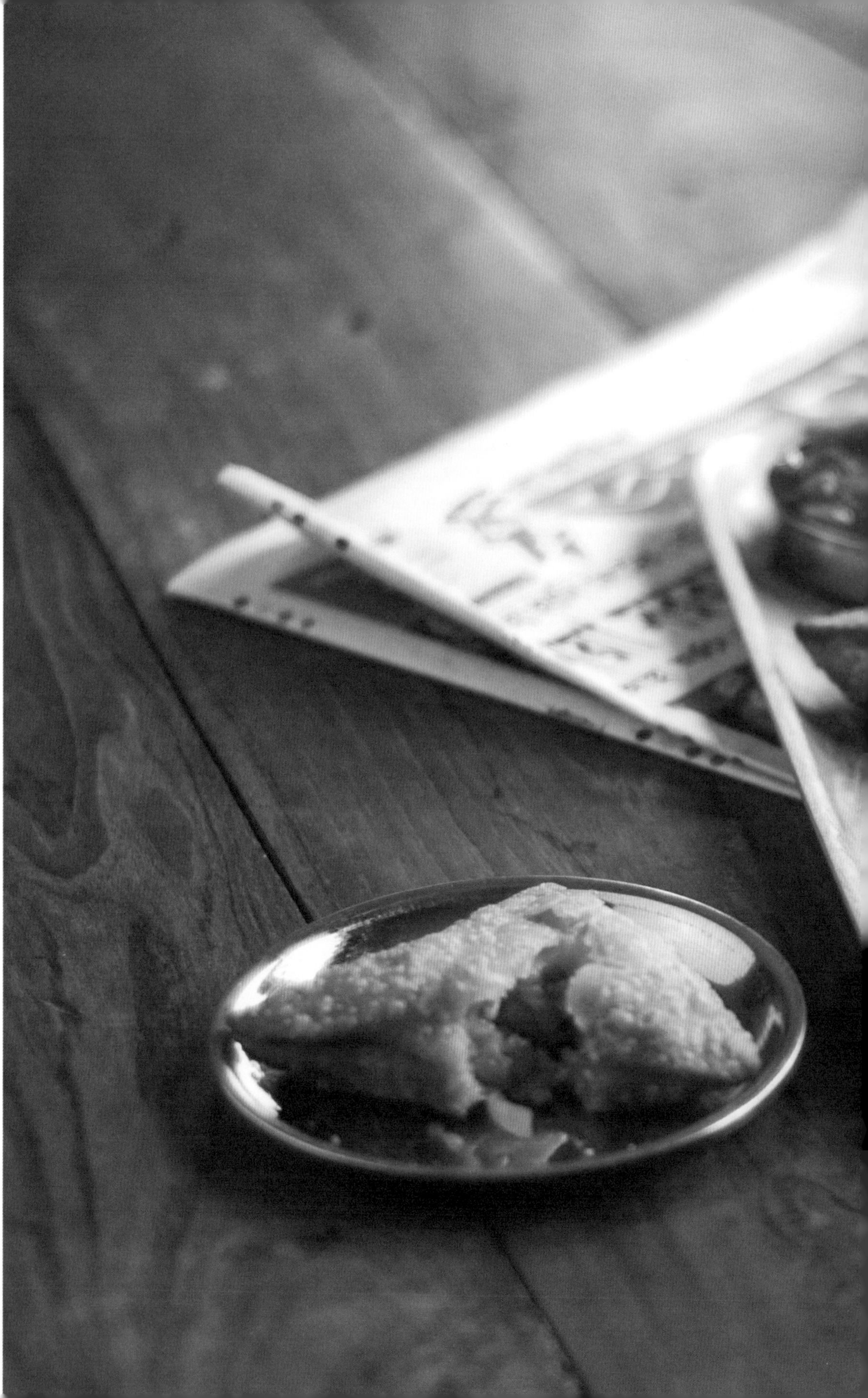

DHALER BORA
LENTIL FRITTERS

Serves 4-6
V, WF, GF

This recipe is based on my mother's and is super addictive. Ground lentils are mixed with onions, green chillies, spices and fresh coriander to make a batter, which is dropped very quickly by hand into hot oil to make these irresistible fritters. If you're around Brick Lane during Ramadhan you'll spot some of the Bangladeshi cafés with their shopfront windows opened up so you can look in on large pans of fritters being fried – a real treat to watch. There's something so comforting about the smell of frying onions and spices that I'm always hard pressed to avoid buying a brown paper bag full of dhaler bora and tucking into them straight away.

200g red split lentils, soaked
  30 minutes
2–3 green chillies, chopped
2 medium onions, quartered
  and finely sliced
1½ teaspoons salt
1 teaspoon ground turmeric
½ teaspoon ground cumin
¼ teaspoon chilli powder
4 heaped tablespoons
  gram flour
3 tablespoons chopped
  coriander

500ml vegetable oil, to deep fry

Drain the lentils and coarsely grind them with the green chillies using a hand blender or food processor. Put the sliced onion into a bowl along with the salt and mix together thoroughly with your hand. Add the turmeric, cumin, chilli powder, gram flour and coriander and scrape in the ground lentil mix. Switch to a spoon and mix thoroughly to form a batter that is loose enough to drop off a spoon – if the mix is too thick, loosen it with a dash of water.

Heat the oil in a wok or frying pan over high heat. Once hot (test with a tiny bit of batter – if it sizzles and floats to the surface, the oil is hot enough), reduce the heat to medium and use your hand to carefully drop small golf ball sized portions into the oil, a dozen or so at a time. You can use a tablespoon instead of your hand if you aren't feeling confident but you won't get the distinct rounded shape.

Reduce the heat to low and cook for six or seven minutes, turning regularly until the fritters are deep golden all over.

Use a slotted spoon to transfer to a dish lined with kitchen paper. Continue cooking in batches until the batter is finished. Serve immediately with some sliced red onions and chopped fresh chillies.

Cook's tip – it's important to keep an eye on the heat as you cook the dhaler bora. Turn heat up to medium-high as you drop the batter into the pan (the temperature drops once the batter falls in); then, once you have a full batch frying, turn the heat to low. This will help them become fully crispy.

TOMATO, CAPER &
RICOTTA CROCHETTES

ENOTECA POMAIO
224 BRICK LANE

Serves 4-6

Crochettes or croquettes are popular all over Italy and are usually served as an antipasto. Recipes vary from region to region, with cheese and potato generally being the main components. The ones on the Enoteca Pomaio menu are cheesy with an intense hit of sun-dried tomatoes, and come served with a dollop of fresh pesto on the side. They're very rich so just one or two will be enough to whet your appetite as a dinner party starter, or make them as part of several small plates for a get-together. Once fried the crispy shells burst open to a soft yet deeply flavoured filling. So delicious!

FOR THE FILLING:

100g sun-dried tomatoes in oil,
  drained
400g ricotta cheese
50g pecorino cheese, grated
35g capers
⅛ teaspoon salt
⅛ teaspoon black pepper

FOR THE COATING:

2 tablespoons plain flour
2 tablespoons fine breadcrumbs
1 medium egg

500ml sunflower oil, to deep fry

Put the sun-dried tomatoes, ricotta, pecorino, capers, salt and black pepper into a food processor and blitz to a coarse paste. If you're doing it by hand, chop the tomatoes and capers very finely and then mix in the other ingredients. Place the mixture in a bowl and knead until it's smooth. Rest in the fridge to firm up for at least 20 minutes – or you can leave it overnight and fry the crochettes the next day.

Once the mixture is firm enough to work with, take golf ball sized pieces and roll between your palms to make traditional oval crochette shapes.

When you are ready to cook, assemble the three step coating. Put the flour on one plate and the breadcrumbs on another, and then beat the egg in a small bowl. Lightly roll each crochette in the flour, dip in the egg mixture and then coat evenly in breadcrumbs, making sure they're well coated so they don't fall to pieces during frying. Heat the oil in a deep pan on medium-high heat. Fry the crochettes in batches until golden all over (three to four minutes) and drain on kitchen paper. Serve immediately.

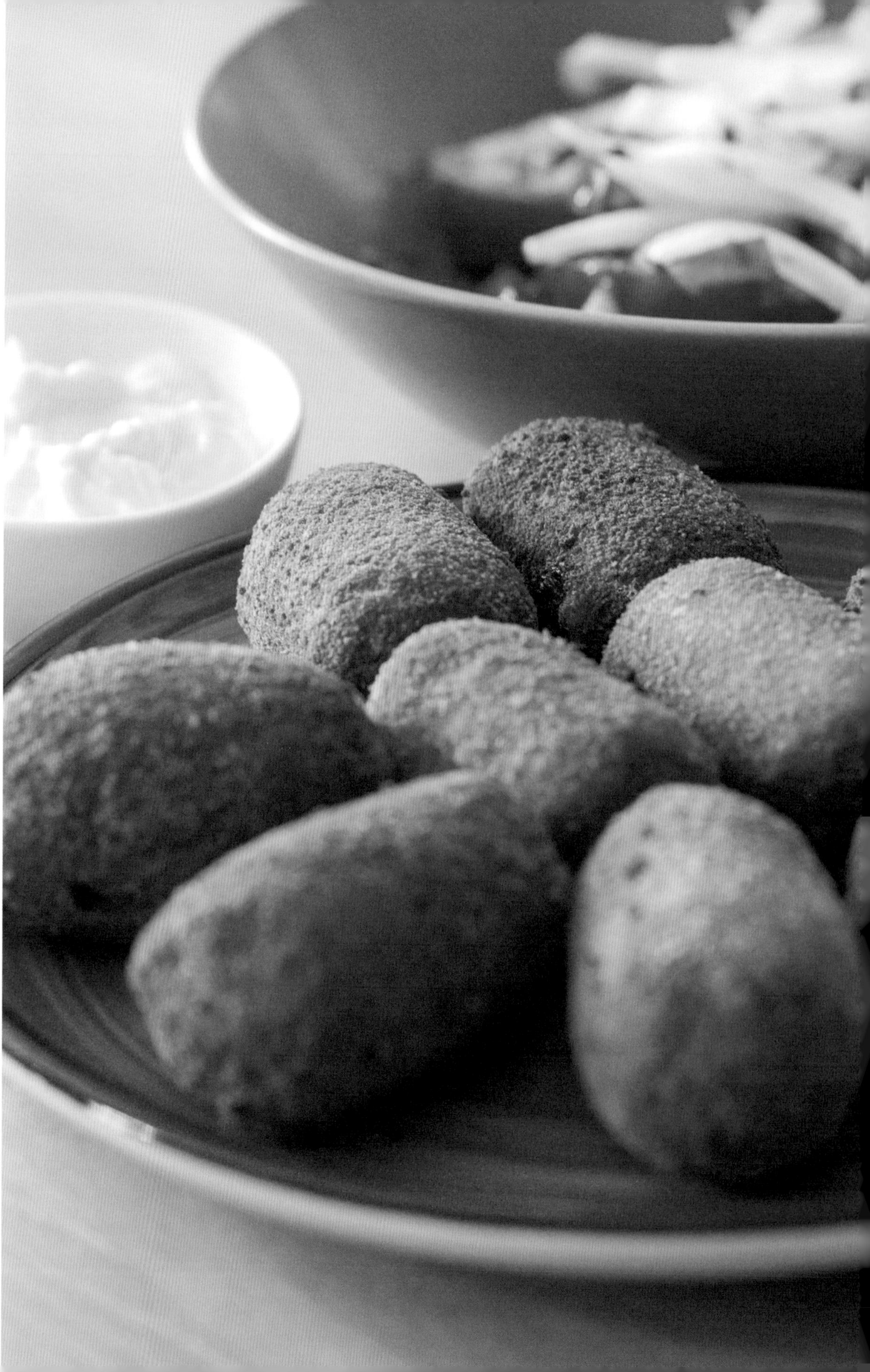

SPINACH & BLACK GARLIC CROQUETTES

LA BUENAVENTURA
BOILER HOUSE
FOOD MARKET

Serves 4-6
V

These vegan croquettes from the La Buenaventura stall make for a great starter or snack: crispy with a melting centre and incredible depth of flavour. Black garlic is white garlic which has been aged over heat for several weeks, turning the cloves black and soft with a sweet, tart flavour – think balsamic mixed with tamarind. It's worth making the effort to find – try www.souschef.co.uk if you can't find it anywhere else. Don't leave out the nutritional yeast either: it adds a lovely umami flavour sometimes lacking in vegan food, and is a great source of vitamin B12. You can find it in most health food stores.

FOR THE FILLING:
4 tablespoons olive oil
1 garlic clove, sliced
150g spinach, finely chopped
½ onion, finely chopped
3 cloves black garlic, sliced
70g plain flour
500ml soy milk
3 tablespoons nutritional yeast
½–1 teaspoon salt
black pepper, to taste

Heat a tablespoon of the olive oil in a frying pan, and fry the sliced garlic until transparent. Add the spinach and a pinch of salt and cook for a few minutes until wilted. Drain any excess water and put the spinach to one side.

Put the remaining olive oil in a medium saucepan and fry the onion and black garlic until soft. Stir in the flour and cook until you have a golden roux, and then slowly add the soy milk to the saucepan, mixing it well with the roux. Once all the soy milk is added, bring the pan to a simmer, stirring until you have a thick white sauce. Don't worry about lumps too much. You can now add the spinach, nutritional yeast, salt and black pepper – mix it well and adjust the seasoning to taste.

Cont...

FOR THE COATING:

150g plain flour
150g breadcrumbs
150ml soy milk

500ml vegetable oil, to deep fry

With a hand blender, blitz the mixture until smooth, and then cook on medium heat for about 15 minutes, stirring regularly to prevent it sticking to the bottom of the pan. You will know it is ready when the mixture comes off the sides of the pan.

Grease a shallow glass or ceramic dish and pour in the mixture. Cover with cling film, making sure it is in contact with the surface to prevent a crust forming. Leave to cool for a few hours or overnight until the filling is cold and firm.

Once the filling is cold, get three shallow bowls and put the coating flour in one, breadcrumbs in another and soy milk in the third. Take a tablespoon of filling and roll it in the flour, and then shape into an oval croquette between your hands. Dip the croquette into the soy milk and roll it in the breadcrumbs. Repeat the process with the remaining filling and let the finished croquettes sit for 30 minutes before frying.

Heat the oil to 175ºC in a deep pan. Fry the croquettes in small batches until golden brown all over (don't do too many at once or you'll lower the oil temperature), then drain on kitchen paper and serve, maybe with some La Beunaventura veganaisse (page 172).

DUCK RILLETTES

CHEZ ELLES
45 BRICK LANE

Serves 6
DF, WF, GF

Reims-born friends Nadia and Lili have created a little Parisian-style bistroquet in the heart of Brick Lane. Once you step inside you could be forgiven for thinking you're in Paris – every detail of the bohemian, chic interior, from colourful tiles to vintage tableware, feels authentically Gallic. The menu of classic French bistro cooking is all freshly cooked using local British produce where possible. These duck rillettes are a standard at the restaurant, and are truly delicious and easy to make – be sure to save the duck fat after cooking to roast potatoes in.

4 bay leaves
6 sprigs thyme
1 star anise
4 cloves garlic, sliced
6 duck legs
1 litre duck fat
salt
black pepper

Preheat your oven to 150°C (130°C fan).

Scatter the bay leaves, thyme, star anise and garlic evenly on the bottom of a roasting tin. Season the duck legs with salt and black pepper and arrange in a layer in the tin. Melt the duck fat in a pan and carefully pour over the top. Cover the roasting tin tightly with foil, then put it in the oven and cook for two and a half hours. It is ready when the meat is falling off the bone – you can check this by pushing the meat with a spoon and seeing if it falls away easily.

Leave to cool, then take the duck legs out of the fat and shred the meat off the bone. Mix a few tablespoons of fat (or more, if you prefer a higher fat content) into the meat to give you a terrine-like consistency. Serve with fresh rustic French bread or sourdough.

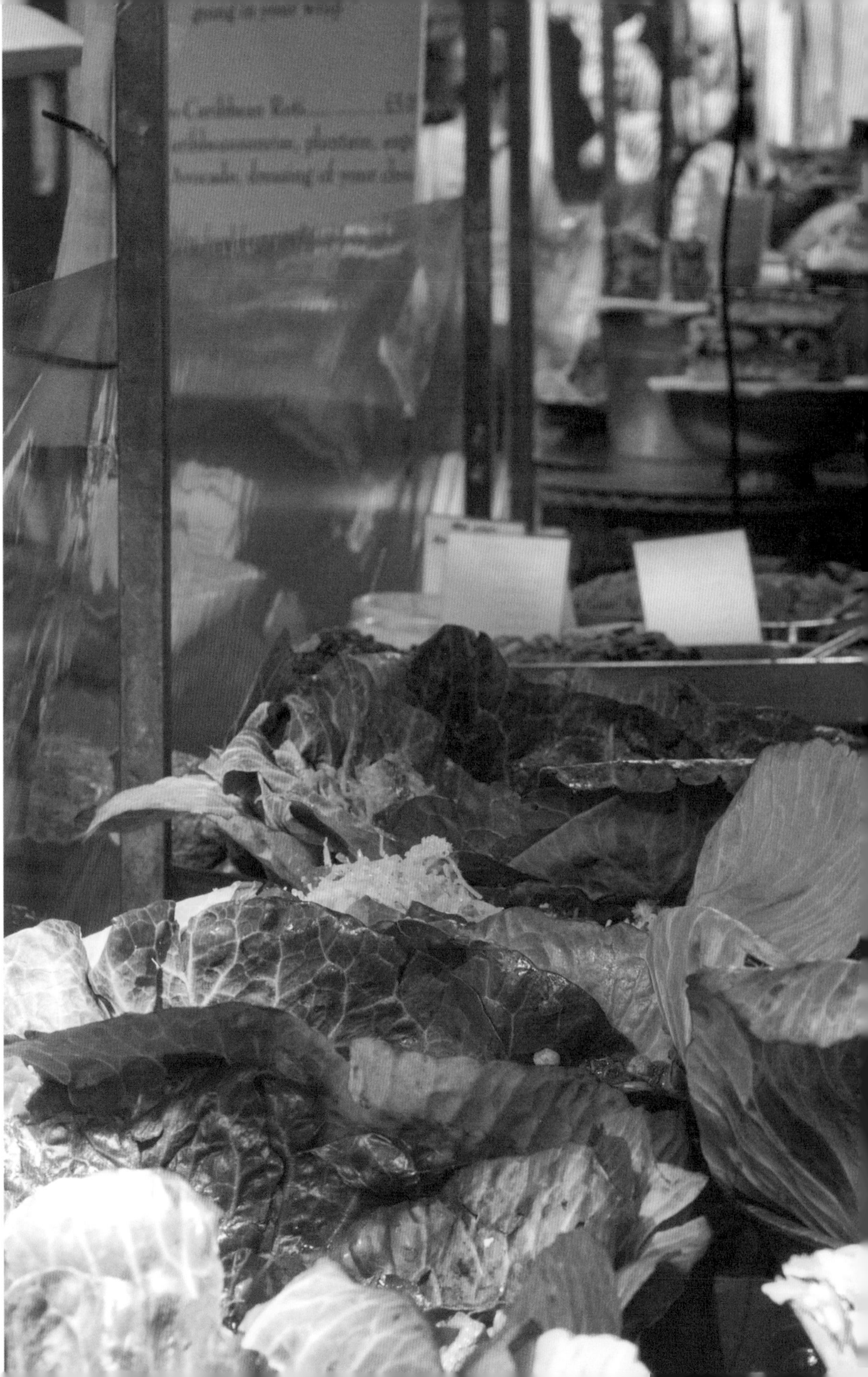

BRUSCHETTA
WITH BROCCOLI, CAULIFLOWER & GUANCIALE

ENOTECA POMAIO
224 BRICK LANE

Serves 4
EF

This trendy Italian restaurant and organic craft wine bar is nestled towards the Shoreditch end of Brick Lane and is the brainchild of brothers Marco and Lacapo Rossi, who wanted to bring flavours of the Tuscan kitchen to East London. Their specialty is modern twists on Italian classics, which chef Simone Barsanti executes to perfection. This bruschetta matches creamy cauliflower and broccoli with crunchy sourdough toast and salty guanciale chips from the Casentino Valley. It is simple but delicious, and easy to vary with the addition of anchovies or cheese. If you're like me and don't eat pork, try replacing the guanciale with grilled turkey rashers.

250g cauliflower,
  roughly chopped
400g broccoli, roughly chopped
100g guanciale, cut into strips
4 slices sourdough bread
50g butter
½ teaspoon chilli flakes
100ml single cream

Cut the cauliflower and broccoli into small florets and blanch in a pan of lightly salted boiling water for a couple of minutes until crisp-tender. Drain in a colander, then rinse with cold water and set aside until the water is drained completely.

Preheat the oven to 170°C (150°C fan). Put the guanciale strips on a baking tray and bake for about eight minutes, making sure to keep an eye on them to avoid burning. Remove and set aside. Increase the temperature to 180°C and put the sourdough bread in the oven for four minutes until it is 'bruschettato' (crunchy and almost burnt).

Melt the butter with the chilli flakes in a frying pan over medium heat, then add the cauliflower and broccoli. Sauté for three minutes, then pour over the cream, give a quick stir and take off the heat. The broccoli and cauliflower should be slightly wilted but still crunchy.

Spoon the broccoli-cauliflower cream onto the pieces of sourdough toast, scatter over the guanciale chips and serve.

BEEF EMPANADAS

MOO CANTINA
62 BRICK LANE

Makes 12

Jose Luis and Hernan conceptualised Moo Cantina as a restaurant that was more 'fun dining' than 'fine dining'. They opened first in nearby Spitalfields, before branching out to Brick Lane. These classic beef empanadas have always been on the menu and are an Argentinian staple – parcels of lightly spiced meat, traditionally finely chopped rather than minced, and mixed with fresh and dried herbs. There's piquancy from the olives and peppers and smokiness from paprika and cumin. Think of our beloved Cornish pasty (which empanadas are said to originate from), then cast your mind to sunnier climes.

FOR THE FILLING:

2 tablespoons olive oil

1 large onion, finely chopped

1 large garlic clove, grated

1 red pepper, deseeded and
  finely chopped

500g sirloin beef fillet,
  finely chopped

1 teaspoon cumin

½ teaspoon sweet paprika

½ teaspoon smoked paprika

1 teaspoon dried oregano

⅔ teaspoon salt

¼ teaspoon black pepper

12–15 Manzanilla olives,
  pitted and chopped

2 tablespoons flat leaf parsley,
  finely chopped

FOR THE PASTRY:

130g unsalted butter, chilled

450g plain flour, plus more
  for dusting

2 teaspoons baking powder

½ teaspoon salt

2 medium eggs

100ml milk

Make your filling first. Heat the oil in a frying pan over medium heat. Throw in the onions, sauté for a couple of minutes until translucent and add the garlic and chopped red pepper. Stir through for a minute, then and add the meat, cumin, sweet and smoked paprika, oregano, salt and black pepper. Cook for around seven minutes, stirring regularly. The meat will release some liquid so once this has almost evaporated add the chopped olives and parsley. Cook for another minute, then turn off the heat. Transfer to a dish and leave to cool completely.

Meanwhile, make the pastry. Cut the butter into small cubes and place in a bowl with the flour, baking powder and salt. Rub between the tips of your fingers until you have a fine breadcrumb-like texture. In a separate bowl whisk one egg with the milk and 50ml cold water. Create a well in the centre of the flour mixture and pour in the wet ingredients. Use your hand to bring everything together to a ball of dough, then wrap in cling film and chill in the fridge.

When you are ready to make your empanadas, preheat your oven to 190°C (170°C fan). Unwrap the pastry and knead for a minute, then divide it into 12 equal pieces. Roll each piece into a 15cm round on a lightly floured surface. Place two tablespoons of filling onto the lower half of each round, leaving a centimetre gap around the edge. Fold over the top half to make a semi-circular pasty, and seal with a little water round the edges. You can either roll up the edges or gently press down with a fork to crimp.

Whisk the remaining egg in a small bowl, and brush the empanadas with it. Put them on a lined baking sheet and bake for 30 minutes, or until golden brown. Serve either hot or cold with chimichurri (page 122) or garlic mayo.

BUFFALO WINGS
WITH BLUE CHEESE DIP

STICKY WINGS
40 BRICK LANE

Serves 4

If you enter Brick Lane from the Aldgate East end you only need to walk a couple of minutes to spot this lovely American-style diner, which has a cult following for its buffalo wings. Owner Darul Rahman worked for several years in the US, learning to make Buffalo wings the proper way. You can tell he's an expert when you try his recipe: crispy, fried wings coated in a buttery, tart and spicy sauce, then served with a pungent blue cheese dip. Franks Red Hot Original Sauce is a crucial component of the dish, giving it a taste of an authentic New York staple in the heart of the East End, or in your home.

FOR THE WINGS:

20 chicken wings, halved
  at the joint
½ tablespoon plain flour
½ teaspoon cayenne pepper
¼ teaspoon salt
⅛ teaspoon black pepper
125g butter, at room
  temperature
½ teaspoon garlic powder
148ml bottle Franks Red
  Hot Original Sauce

500ml vegetable oil, to deep fry

FOR THE BLUE CHEESE DIP:

150g soured cream
150g mayonnaise
75g blue cheese, crumbled

Place the wings in a bowl and sprinkle over the plain flour, cayenne pepper, salt and pepper. Toss together to make sure every piece is coated, then place in the fridge for 20 minutes.

Heat the vegetable oil to 190°C in a deep pan or a fryer and fry the wings in batches for about 12 minutes, or until golden. While the chicken is frying, make your hot sauce. Melt the butter in a pan over medium heat. Once it has melted, add the garlic powder and the entire bottle of Frank's Red Hot Sauce and swirl around in the pan to mix. Set aside.

Drain the fried wings on kitchen paper, then toss them in the pan of hot sauce until all the pieces are well coated. Mix together the soured cream, mayonnaise and blue cheese in a bowl and serve with the buffalo wings.

LAMB KOFTAS

Serves 4-6
DF, WF, GF, EF

When I was young my dad would take me along to the Sunday market on Brick Lane and treat me to lunch at Sweet & Spicy, a corner café specialising in unfussy Pakistani food. We'd always have their kebab rolls – finely ground, spiced minced lamb cooked on skewers and served inside a soft flatbread. The kebabs were served with their famous red sauce – which was sweet and spicy! Sadly the place has closed down now; however anyone who has craved comforting Pakistani food on Brick Lane will remember them with nostalgia. These koftas are inspired by Sweet & Spicy and are my version of a simple lunchtime staple which doesn't skimp on flavour.

1 medium onion, grated
1 tablespoon ginger, grated
4 cloves garlic, chopped
4 green chillies, chopped
2 tablespoons chopped
  fresh coriander
1 teaspoon chilli powder
1 teaspoon ground coriander
1 teaspoon salt
½ teaspoon ground cumin
½ teaspoon ground turmeric
600g minced lamb

150ml vegetable oil,
  to shallow fry

Put the onion, ginger, garlic, chillies, fresh coriander, chilli powder, ground coriander, salt, cumin and turmeric into a blender with plenty of freshly ground black pepper. Quickly blitz to get a coarse paste. Scrape the paste into a bowl, add the mince and mix well with your hands. Divide the mixture into 16 portions and gently roll each one into a ball between your palms. Flatten each slightly, and put on a plate.

Heat the oil in a frying pan and, once hot, reduce the heat to medium-low. Gently slide a few koftas at a time into the oil and cook for four or five minutes on each side until golden brown. Use a slotted spoon to transfer the cooked koftas to a warm dish, then repeat until they're all done. These are best served hot with some freshly baked naan bread or chapatti, salad, a good dollop of raita and a spicy hot sauce to recreate those Sweet & Spicy kebab roll memories! A sprinkling of pomegranate seeds and a wedge of lemon also add a lovely touch.

JAGGERY, GINGER & CHILLI LAMB CHOPS

Serves 4-6
EF, DF

Jaggery, also known as *gur*, is a wonderful unrefined sugar, made from palm sap or sugar cane juice and then set into solid blocks or rounds. You can easily get hold of it at Asian grocery stores and some larger supermarkets – Taj Stores on Brick Lane stock a good selection. In Asian cooking jaggery is used in both sweet and savoury dishes and adds a lovely bold, fudgy taste. This recipe features one of my favourite flavour combinations – sweet and spicy. Juicy pieces of lamb chops spend the night in an intense marinade before being roasted. As the jaggery slowly caramelises in the oven, it adds a delicious sweetness. Thinner cuts of lamb chops are ideal here as the there is more surface area to absorb the flavours of the marinade and crisp up in the oven. Great paired with drinks, or served as a main with my spicy roast potatoes (page 145).

1kg lamb chops

1½ teaspoons salt

¼ teaspoon black pepper

juice of 1 lime

6 tablespoons jaggery

5cm piece of ginger, peeled and roughly chopped

5 large dried red chillies

2 tablespoons vegetable oil

1 teaspoon wholegrain mustard

Mix the lamb in a bowl with the salt, pepper and lime juice and set aside. Put the jaggery in a blender with the ginger, chillies, vegetable oil and mustard and blitz to a coarse paste – you could also use a pestle and mortar. Scrape the paste onto the lamb chops and mix thoroughly, ensuring all the meat is evenly covered. Cover the bowl with cling film or transfer to a container with a lid and leave in the fridge to marinate for at least three hours, preferably overnight, to give the flavours time to develop.

When you are ready to cook the chops, preheat the oven to 220°C (200°C fan). Spread out the chops on a baking tray and put them on the highest shelf in the oven. Roast for 35 to 45 minutes, turning two or three times and basting with the excess marinade. Serve hot.

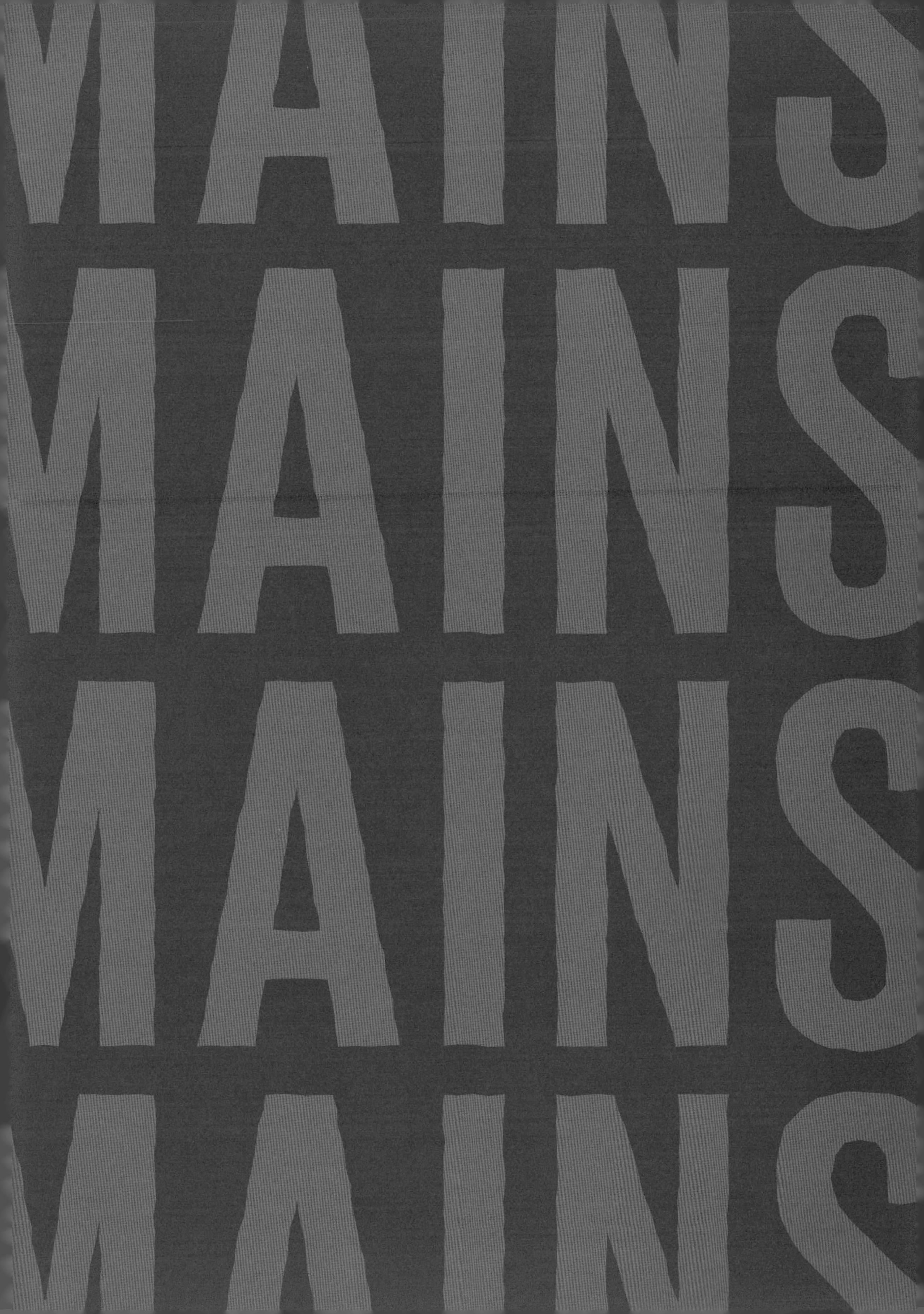
MAINS
MAINS
MAINS
MAINS

FRIED PANEER
WITH PEPPERS & CHILLI

Serves 4
WF, GF, EF

If you've never tried paneer then prepare to be pleasantly surprised. It's a solid, neutral-tasting Indian cheese which carries flavour really well. It's usually on the menus of the famous Brick Lane curry houses but not cooked the way I'd have it at home. Here I've coated paneer cubes in a light, spiced batter, then fried them until golden before simmering gently in a flavourful tomato, spring onion and pepper sauce. The dish is a great showcase for the aromatic Bengali five-spice mix panch phoron as you can really taste the individual spices.

500g paneer
4 tablespoons cornflour
½ teaspoon chilli powder
¼ teaspoon black pepper
2 tablespoons oil
1 teaspoon sesame oil
½ teaspoon panch phoron
2 cloves garlic, finely grated
4 spring onions, chopped
2 green chillies, chopped
2 teaspoons brown sugar
¼ teaspoon turmeric
1 teaspoon paprika
2 tomatoes, chopped
1 green pepper, chopped
1 red pepper, chopped
2 tablespoons chopped
  fresh coriander
salt

Chop the paneer into 2cm cubes and place into a bowl. Sprinkle over the cornflour, chilli powder, black pepper and about half a teaspoon of salt and toss together, then add two tablespoons of water and gently stir so all the paneer cubes are coated. Heat a wok or deep frying pan on medium-high and add the oil. Carefully slide in the paneer pieces and fry, turning regularly with a spatula, for about two minutes or until they are golden all over. Remove the paneer and set aside.

To the same pan, add the sesame oil and panch phoron. Once the spices begin to pop (about 30 seconds) add the garlic and gently brown. Next, throw in the spring onions, chillies, sugar, turmeric, paprika and half a teaspoon of salt. Stir for a minute, then add the tomatoes and peppers. Cover and cook for five minutes, then add the fried paneer back into the pan and stir though. Pour in 100ml hot water, cover and turn the heat to low. Cook for another seven or eight minutes. Stir in the fresh coriander and turn off the heat. Serve with chapatti, or rice.

BUTTERNUT SQUASH
WITH CORIANDER & CHILLIES

Serves 4-6
V, WF, GF

Root vegetables such as pumpkin and butternut squash are really popular in Bangladesh, and the Bengali grocery stores around Brick Lane display a choice selection whenever they're in season. This recipe is a staple Bengali dish often served alongside meat or chicken, but it is equally popular on its own as it is quite substantial and satisfying – great for vegetarians. Sweet butternut squash cubes are gently cooked with cumin and turmeric and finished with a burst of fresh coriander and sliced green chillies. It's one of those recipes that I cook again and again as it's super easy and ready in about 20 minutes.

2 tablespoons oil
1 small onion, finely sliced
¾ teaspoon salt
1 bay leaf
1 teaspoon ground turmeric
1 teaspoon ground cumin
700g butternut squash, peeled
  and chopped into large chunks
2–3 green chillies,
  slit lengthways
2 tablespoons chopped
  coriander

Heat the oil in a wok or deep frying pan on medium-high heat, then add the onions, salt and bay leaf. Sauté for a few minutes until the onion is translucent but not browned. Add the turmeric and cumin, cook for a minute and then add the butternut squash, ensuring all the pieces are coated in the spice.

Add 100ml of boiling water and bring to a gentle simmer, then throw the green chillies on top and reduce the heat to low. Cover and cook for eight to ten minutes, or until the squash cubes are soft and tender but still retaining their shape. Very gently stir in the chopped coriander and check the seasoning. Cover and cook for another minute before turning off the heat. I like to serve this with steamed rice or flatbread for a simple lunch, or as a side to other Asian dishes.

MUSHROOM SHAWARMA

CAFÉ 1001
91 BRICK LANE

Serves 6
V, WF, GF

A wonderful vegan and vegetarian option that is great on a pitta with salad and a dollop of garlic mayo. The spices perfectly complement the mushrooms and you get a hint of sour from the sumac. A delicious meat-free Monday dish with minimal prep and only 15 minutes of oven time.

2 teaspoons ground cumin

1½ teaspoons paprika

¾ teaspoons ground coriander

½ teaspoon ground cardamom

½ teaspoon ground cinnamon

½ teaspoon ground turmeric

1½ tablespoons sumac

juice of ½ lemon

6 cloves garlic, finely grated

40g ginger, finely grated

50g fresh coriander, stems
 and leaves, chopped

6 large portobello mushrooms

salt

black pepper

Heat a frying pan on medium heat and toast the cumin, paprika, coriander, cardamom, cinnamon and turmeric for about 30 seconds, stirring continuously. Take off the heat and put the spices into a bowl. Add the sumac, lemon juice, garlic, ginger, chopped coriander and olive oil and mix well. Season to taste with salt and black pepper.

Wipe the mushrooms clean, then add them to the marinade and stir through so that they are evenly coated. Leave to marinate overnight in the fridge. When you are ready to cook the mushrooms, preheat the oven to 180°C (160°C fan). Lay the mushrooms on a baking tray and bake for around 15 minutes until lightly golden. Serve hot.

MOUSSAKA

DAMASCU BITE
119-121
BRICK LANE

Serves 4-6
V, WF, GF

Damascu Bite originally opened in Spitalfields and moved to Brick Lane ten years ago. They create hearty, Syrian home-cooking with simple dishes made with love and attention. As well as their succulent shawarmas and grilled meats, they specialise in vegetarian dishes which cater to the growing vegetarian and vegan clientele. Damascu Bite's moussaka is unlike the well-known Greek moussaka and the similarity ends at the inclusion of aubergines. The dish is vegan and one of their popular offerings, simple to put together, packed full of flavour and even better the next day! The secret to a good moussaka, the chef tells me, is slowly sautéing the onion and peppers and really taking your time over them, so that you have perfectly translucent, tender veggies which are not deeply browned. The more aubergine the better so if you have an extra handful add it in. Pair this dish with a fresh, citrusy tabbouleh (page 167) for a wonderfully filling and light meal.

200ml oil
8 cloves garlic, chopped
500g onions, halved and
  finely sliced
1 medium red pepper, chopped
1 medium orange pepper,
  chopped
2 teaspoons black pepper
1–2 tablespoons salt,
  or according to taste

Heat the oil on medium heat in a deep, wide pan and add the garlic, onions and peppers. Sauté for 20 to 30 minutes until translucent and perfectly soft but not browned. Make sure to keep an eye on the pan, and turn the heat to low if the onions begin to colour too much. Stir in the black pepper and salt, then add chopped tomatoes and simmer for ten minutes until you have a medium consistency sauce. Check and adjust the seasoning to taste, then set aside. Preheat the oven to 180°C.

While the sauce is cooking, take a potato peeler and peel the aubergine in large strips, ensuring you take off about three-quarters of the skin.

4 x 400g tins chopped tomatoes
  (or 1.5kg fresh tomatoes,
  blanched, peeled
  and chopped)
2 medium aubergines
1 x 400g tin chickpeas
1 tablespoon ground cumin

500ml vegetable oil, to deep fry

33cm x 23cm baking dish or tin

Too much of the skin imparts a bitter taste but a little adds texture. Chop into 2cm chunks. Heat the vegetable oil in a deep-sided pan or wok, then deep fry the aubergine for three or four minutes, or until golden brown all over. Drain well on kitchen paper.

Now assemble your moussaka. Take the baking dish and put the fried aubergine in an even layer on the bottom. Drain and rinse the chickpeas, place in a small bowl and coarsely mash with a fork. Spread the mash evenly over the aubergine and sprinkle the ground cumin on top. Finish with a layer of the tomato sauce and, if you like, add a few slices of fresh tomato and some chopped peppers on top.

Bake for 40 to 45 minutes, until golden on top. Serve with tabbouleh and some pitta bread, or with some grilled meats.

SWEET POTATO & AUBERGINE CURRY

Serves 4-6
V, WF, GF

If, like me, you are a fan of slightly sweet and hot flavours, then this curry will hit just the spot. Although potatoes and aubergine are often cooked together in Indian and Bengali cooking, sweet potato offers a unique twist. Again, panch photon or Bengali five spice is a star ingredient with its combination of seeds including mustard, fenugreek, nigella, cumin and fennel – a winning blend of aromas!

1 large sweet potato

1 large aubergine

4 tablespoons oil

2 teaspoons panch phoron

1 garlic clove, grated

1 medium red onion,
  finely sliced

1 bay leaf

1 teaspoon salt

½ teaspoon ground turmeric

1½ teaspoons ground cumin

1 teaspoon ground coriander

1 teaspoon chilli powder

1 teaspoon garam masala

2 whole green chillies
  (or chop them for extra heat)

2 large tomatoes, chopped

3–4 tablespoons chopped
  fresh coriander

First peel and wash the sweet potato, then chop into 2cm chunks. Wash the aubergine and chop into 2cm chunks and set aside. Heat the oil in a large pan over medium heat and add the panch phoron. Wait until the seeds begin to pop, then add the garlic, sliced onion, bay leaf and salt.

Sauté for about five minutes, until the onions are translucent and lightly browned, then add the turmeric, cumin, ground coriander, chilli powder and garam masala. Reduce the heat to low and cook for about two minutes until the spices are cooked. Stir in the sweet potatoes, aubergine and green chillies. Add the chopped tomatoes, cover with a lid and cook on low heat for ten minutes. Give everything a stir and check that it's not sticking to the bottom, then add 200ml water, cover and cook for another ten minutes.

The curry is done once the potatoes are soft enough to be pierced by a fork. Sprinkle over the chopped coriander and cook for about another minute before you take the pan off the heat. Serve with rice or flatbread.

COCONUT PRAWNS

Serves 4
WF, GF, DF, EF

Fish and seafood are staples in Bangladeshi cuisine. For many of the immigrant population who moved to the East End a good fish/seafood selection is a pre-requisite for any good grocery store. Most of the produce is frozen as it's imported from Bangladesh but you can use fresh British prawns here and the flavour won't be compromised. This is a lovely recipe: simple to make, flavourful and lightly fragrant. The coconut milk gives the dish a creamy sweetness and mustard seeds, a classic Bengali companion to seafood, add a little punch. So good poured over a mound of freshly steamed basmati rice.

400g raw prawns, peeled
  and de-veined
½ teaspoon ground turmeric
2 tablespoons vegetable oil
1 teaspoon mustard seeds
2 cloves garlic, grated
1 small onion, finely chopped
⅔ teaspoon salt
1 teaspoon chilli powder
1 teaspoon ground coriander
300ml coconut milk
4 whole green chillies
2 tablespoons chopped
  fresh coriander

Firstly rinse the prawns and dab dry with kitchen paper. Place in a bowl and sprinkle with half the turmeric and mix. Heat the oil in a pan on medium heat and lightly fry the prawns for around 30 seconds on each side. Scoop the prawns out and reserve.

Add the mustard seeds to the same pan. When they start to pop, add the crushed garlic and fry for a minute or two, then add the onions and salt. Sauté for a couple of minutes, until the onions have softened.

Add the remaining turmeric, chilli powder and ground coriander and cook for a minute, then pour in the coconut milk and whole green chillies. Bring the sauce up to a simmer, then put the fried prawns back in the pan. Cover and cook for five minutes and stir in the chopped fresh coriander just before turning off the heat. Serve with rice.

PRAWNS & POTOL

Serves 4-6
WF, GF, DF, EF

Potol or pointed gourd is an unusual vegetable popular in Bangladeshi cooking. When cooked it tastes somewhere between cucumber, spinach and broccoli – both fresh and earthy at the same time. The best thing is that they are perennial, though more common during summer and autumn time. You can easily pick up a portion from Taj Stores on Brick Lane if you live in East London, or try your local Asian supermarket. This is a classic way of eating them: fresh tasting and fairly dry, so it works great with steamed basmati rice and a simple salad.

600g potol

300g raw king prawns, peeled and de-veined

80ml vegetable oil

6 cloves garlic, grated

1 small onion, finely sliced

1 teaspoon salt

2 teaspoons chilli powder

1 teaspoon ground turmeric

2 teaspoon ground coriander

1 teaspoon ground cumin

4 green chillies, cut lengthways

2 tablespoons chopped fresh coriander

Rinse the potol and prepare them by top and tailing, then slice lengthways and set aside. Rinse the prawns.

Heat the oil in a frying pan on medium heat, then add the garlic and sauté until golden. Add the onion and salt and cook four or five minutes until just starting to colour. Stir in the chilli powder, turmeric, ground coriander and cumin and cook for a minute, then tip in the prawns and mix, ensuring they are coated evenly in the masala. Cover and cook for three to four minutes, until they're about half cooked. Give the prawns a stir, then throw in the potol and chillies and mix. Cover and cook on a low heat for ten minutes, stirring halfway. The potol should be tender and still holding their shape. Add the chopped coriander, give everything a final stir through and turn off the flame.

Serve hot with a squeeze of lime and basmati rice.

PAN-FRIED TILAPIA
WITH FRIED ONIONS

Serves 4
GF, DF, WF, EF

For a jazzed-up fish Friday try this easy dish, inspired by Gram Bangla and Banglar Mukh, a couple of the smaller Bangladeshi eateries on Brick Lane which specialise in home-style cooking. These restaurants tend to have only a few meat or chicken dishes, but when it comes to fish you're spoilt for choice with a vast selection of dishes which are fried, curried and/or made into dumplings. This fish recipe is crispy and fragrant and so good with simple steamed rice. Best of all it's on your plate in about ten minutes.

4 tilapia fillets, without skin

2 teaspoons salt

1 teaspoon ground turmeric

½ teaspoon ground cumin

½ teaspoon chilli powder

2 onions, finely sliced

2 tablespoons chopped
  fresh coriander

2 green chillies, cut lengthways

250ml vegetable oil,
  to shallow fry

Pat dry your tilapia fillets and place on a large, flat dish. Mix the salt with the turmeric, cumin and chilli powder in a small bowl and rub about a teaspoon into each fillet. Make sure to cover both sides evenly and set aside. Put 150ml of oil in a pan over high heat and add the sliced onions. Fry them for six to eight minutes, or until golden and slightly crispy. Stir through the chopped coriander and green chillies a minute before taking off the heat. Use a slotted spoon to transfer the onions to a dish.

Next, heat 100ml of oil in a clean frying pan over medium-high heat. When the oil is very hot, carefully slide two tilapia fillets at a time into the pan and fry for five minutes on each side, until golden brown. Remove to a warm dish and repeat with the remaining two fillets. Serve the fish with steamed rice, topped with some of the fried onions

Cook's tip – it is important to heat up the oil properly before you put the fish in so it immediately begins to crisp up. Don't be tempted to turn the fish over too early, and when you do, make sure to use a large, flat spatula.

COD WITH MANGETOUT

Serves 4
GF, DF, WF, EF

This simple fish curry in a light gravy is based on a classic Bengali dish made with a bony fish called rui, popular in Bengali homes and home-style eateries like Gram Bangla in Brick Lane. I use cod instead of rui as it's boneless, but otherwise I keep to the same flavours and spices. Bengali fish recipes usually begin by cooking the vegetables, adding the fish towards the end of cooking. However, European mangetout are more delicate than the Bangladeshi kind called uri and cook quicker, so in this version they go in the pan after the fish. If you can find uri then add them after the spices and cook for five minutes with the lid on before adding the fish.

2 tablespoons oil

3 cloves garlic, sliced

1 small onion, finely chopped

1½ teaspoons salt

1 teaspoon ground turmeric

1 teaspoon chilli powder

1 teaspoon ground coriander

450g cod fillet, cut into
  bite-sized pieces

300g mangetout or Bangladeshi
  uri, halved

3 green chillies, cut lengthways

2 tablespoons chopped
  fresh coriander

Heat the oil over medium heat in a saucepan and add the garlic. When the garlic has browned add the onion and salt and sauté for two to three minutes until the onion is translucent. Pour in a dash of water, then cover and simmer for another 5 minutes until the water separates from the oil – keep an eye on it in case it becomes too dry. Add the turmeric, chilli powder and ground coriander and stir for a couple of minutes until the spices have cooked through and become fragrant.

Add the cod and quickly but gently stir through so that all the pieces are coated in the masala, then cover and cook on low heat for five minutes. The cod should have turned slightly opaque and will be almost cooked through. Place the mangetout on top of the fish – don't stir or the fish will break.

Add enough water to just cover the fish and mangetout and throw in the chillies. Gently shake the pan so that the fish pieces do not catch at the bottom. Cover and simmer for another five minutes, adding the chopped coriander just before taking off the heat.

Serve with steamed rice and a squeeze of lime.

SALMON BUSHI

THE BIG BUSHI
STREET FOOD
MARKET

Serves 6
EF

Mexico meets Japan in these sensational salmon sushi 'burritos'. Khaled Damash started The Big Bushi stall in early 2017 and since then he and his friends have been serving up these giant sushi rolls to the hungry market-goers craving something a little different. This recipe requires minimal cooking – just a bit of prep and you're literally ready to roll and take a bite of your burrito. You'll need a sushi mat and most of the ingredients are available at a large supermarket (though it's more fun to take a trip to Chinatown).

360g Japanese sushi-grade rice
35ml rice vinegar
1 tablespoon agave syrup
1 teaspoon salt
6 sheets nori
125g cream cheese
125g iceberg lettuce, sliced

FOR THE ROAST PEPPER SALSA:
½ red pepper
1 small jalapeño pepper,
  finely chopped

Wash the rice three or four times and put in a pan with 540ml water. Leave to soak for about 20 minutes, then bring to a fierce boil. Reduce the heat to low, cover and cook for another ten minutes, or until all the water has been absorbed and the rice is cooked. In a separate pan bring the rice vinegar, agave syrup and salt to the boil, then set aside to cool. Once the rice is cool stir in the vinegar mixture evenly.

Preheat your oven to 200°C (180°C fan). Put your red pepper cut-side-down on a baking tray and roast for 35 to 40 minutes or until the skin is charred. Cool completely, then peel off the skin, remove the seeds and finely chop the flesh. Add this to a bowl along with the jalapeño. Mix and set aside.

FOR THE SALMON:

480g fresh Scottish salmon

1 tablespoon wasabi paste

2 tablespoons soy sauce

2 teaspoons white sesame seeds

2 teaspoons black sesame seeds

FOR THE AVOCADO:

2 avocados, peeled and pitted

100g daikon (white radish)

zest and juice of 1 lime

FOR THE SALSA ROJA:

1 small guajillo chilli

2 tomatoes

½ small onion, finely chopped

2–3 tablespoons fresh coriander, chopped

½ garlic clove, grated

Cut the salmon into small one centimetre cubes and marinate with the wasabi, soy sauce and sesame seeds. Set aside.

Cut the avocado into thin slices and put in a bowl. Using a potato peeler, make shavings out of the daikon and add to the avocado with the lime juice and zest. Toss gently to mix.

Next, make your salsa roja. Halve the guajillo chilli lengthways, and de-seed. Put the chilli halves with the tomatoes on a baking tray and grill under a high heat for a few minutes until just charred. Leave to cool, then put in a blender with the onions, fresh coriander and garlic and blitz until smooth.

Now assemble your salmon bushi! Place your nori sheet on top of your sushi mat and spread a layer of rice all over it, leaving a space of about 3cm along the top. Spoon two to three tablespoons of the roasted red pepper mix in a horizontal line across the middle of the rice, then put the same amount of the avocado mix on top of that, and of salsa roja on top again. Spoon or pipe a thick line of cream cheese along the bottom of the pile, then lay two to three tablespoons of salmon on top. Add some lettuce and roll with your sushi mat as tightly as you can to create a great big sushi roll. Repeat for the remaining rolls. Cut each bushi in half to serve.

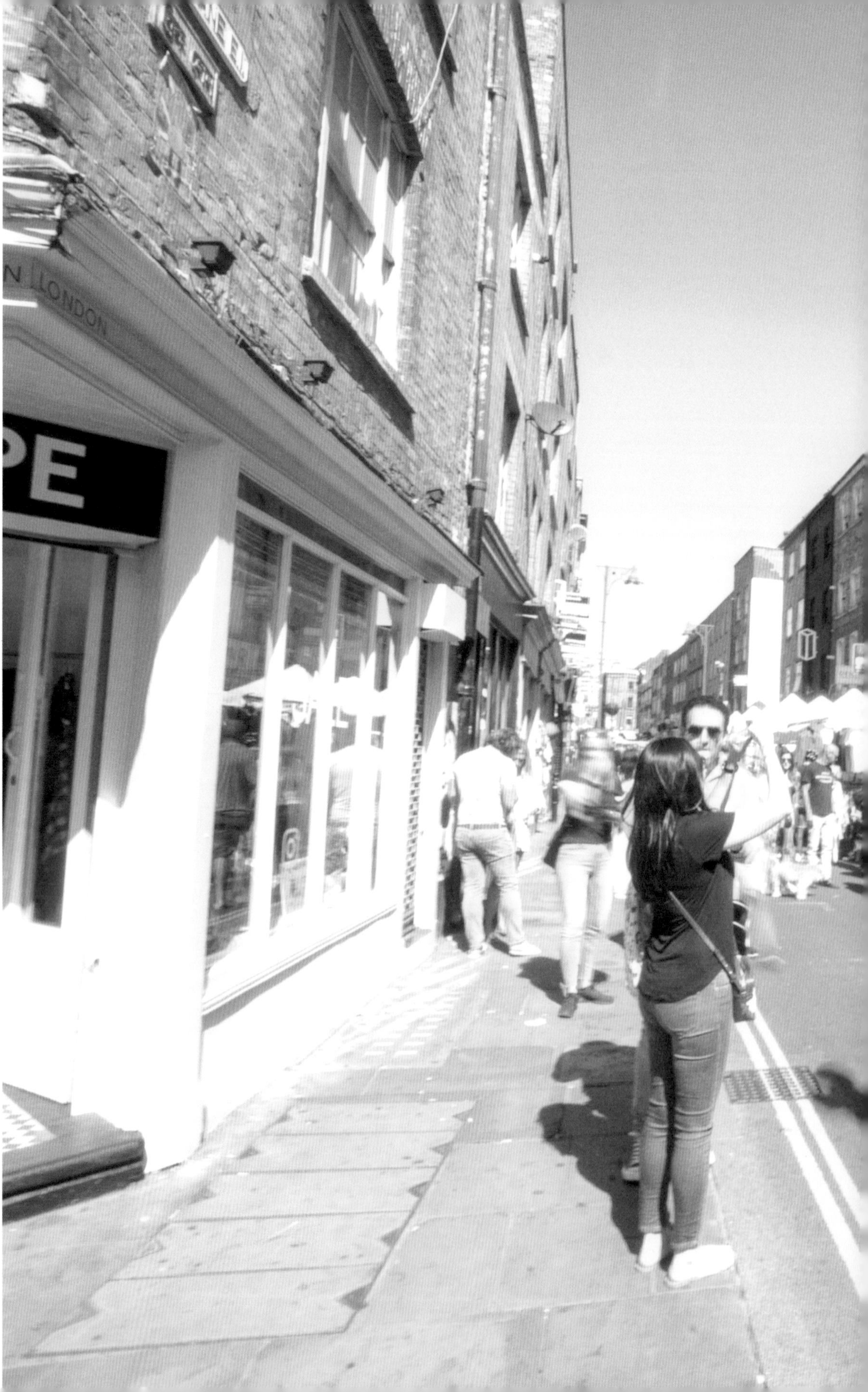
LONDON
PE

CHICKEN & MATZO DUMPLING SOUP

BEIGEL SHOP
155 BRICK LANE

Serves 6
DF

Chicken soup is a favourite the world over in all its various forms and combinations, but this recipe is for the classic Jewish version with added matzo dumplings. Traditionally eaten on the Sabbath and well known for being 'Jewish penicillin', it would slip down the sorest throat and is both wonderfully tasty and extremely nourishing. You can of course leave out the dumplings for a lighter meal, but I don't recommend it – they soak up all the flavours of the soup and become dense and savoury and delicious.

FOR THE SOUP:

1 small chicken
1 small onion, chopped
5 medium carrots, sliced
1 small parsnip, chopped
1 stick celery, chopped
½ bunch fresh dill, chopped
1½ teaspoons salt
½ teaspoon pepper
2 cloves garlic, crushed

FOR THE MATZO DUMPLINGS:

150g matzo meal (or matzo
  crackers, finely ground)
3 medium eggs
2 tablespoons vegetable oil
1 teaspoon salt
¼ teaspoon pepper

Place the chicken into a large casserole dish, breast down.
Add the onion, carrots, parsnip, celery, dill, salt and pepper
and pour in enough water to cover the chicken and vegetables
by about five centimetres.

Bring to a boil over medium-low heat and simmer, partially
covered, for two hours. Skim any fat from the top of the soup
and add the crushed garlic, then partially cover again and
simmer for a further hour or so.

Meanwhile make the dumplings by mixing the matzo meal,
eggs, oil, salt and pepper with two tablespoons of stock from
the pot. Chill in the fridge for about 20 minutes.

When the chicken is very soft and fall-off-the-bone tender, turn
off the heat. Cool slightly, then take out the chicken and set aside.
Pass the soup through a fine sieve to separate the vegetables
– set them aside.

Return the clear broth back to the pot over high heat and bring
to a boil. Add back some of the vegetables.

Shape the matzo mixture into about 12 balls with wet hands to keep
the dough from sticking. Drop the matzo balls one by one into the
boiling broth. Cover with a lid and cook for 20 to 25 minutes.

While the matzo balls are cooking, take the chicken meat off the
bones. Shred the chicken and add back to the soup, then warm
through for a few minutes and serve.

CHICKEN KORMA

Chicken korma cooked at home is unlike any restaurant version (which I would never eat). Originating from Mughlai cuisine, a real korma is rich, decadent and very special. It's usually made with a mixture of whole spices, yoghurt and ghee, and cooked slowly to create a depth of flavour you really can't get in a hurry. There are none of the colourings or sugar you get when you order the curry house version. Sometimes a little nut paste is added which makes the dish even more opulent and perfect for feasting. There are many variations of korma across the Indian subcontinent and I've based mine on the ones I've grown up eating. I use Greek yoghurt for a mellow, creamy flavour, less tangy than natural yoghurt. Whole green chillies are used for fragrance instead of heat so don't be tempted to cut them as korma is meant to be mild. I find that a mixture of thigh and breast meat gives the best result, but you can use one or the other if you prefer.

6 garlic cloves, roughly chopped

5cm piece ginger,
  roughly chopped

100ml oil

2 tablespoons ghee

1 teaspoon panch phoron

3 medium onions, finely sliced

1½ teaspoons salt

3 dried red chillies

2 bay leaves

8 cardamom pods

4 cloves

Crush the garlic and ginger together in a mortar and pestle. Heat the oil and ghee in a large pan on medium-high heat and add the garlic, ginger and panch phoron. After a minute add the onions, salt, dried red chillies, bay leaves, cardamom, cloves, black peppercorns, cinnamon sticks and star anise and sauté until golden – around ten minutes. Add 200ml water, cover and simmer on low heat for 20 to 25 minutes, until the onions have broken up and the oil has separated.

6 black peppercorns

2 cinnamon sticks

1 star anise

1⅓ tablespoons ground cumin

1⅓ tablespoons ground
coriander

½ teaspoon chilli powder

⅛ teaspoon ground turmeric

800g skinless chicken breast
and thigh meat, chopped into
bite-size pieces

300g Greek yoghurt

6 whole green chillies

Keep checking regularly and if the mixture gets too dry or catches at the bottom of the pan add a dash of water and continue cooking.

At this point stir in the cumin, coriander, chilli powder and turmeric and turn up the heat to medium. Cook for two to three minutes until the spices are fragrant and have separated from the oil. If the mixture gets too dry, add a dash of water so the spices don't burn then cover and cook for a few minutes. Now take the chicken pieces and add them to the pan. Stir this around for a couple of minutes to seal the meat, then cover and cook for ten minutes, checking now and then to make sure nothing's burning. Towards the end of the ten minutes you'll notice the chicken releasing moisture – which indicates that it's almost fully cooked.

Take the pan off the heat, wait for a minute and then gradually add the yoghurt, a little at a time so it doesn't curdle. Finally, toss in the green chillies, return the pan to a very low heat and simmer for another eight to ten minutes, stirring occasionally, until the chicken is tender and the gravy is thick and silky. Serve with my easy pilau rice with peas (page 138).

Cook's tip – to ensure the very best korma it is absolutely essential that you take your time over the onions. They should slowly soften, until they almost caramelise and disintegrate. Add a dash of water now and then if they brown too quickly and be patient!

PAI-NGAPI SHAN-STYLE BLACK BEAN CHICKEN

SOE BURMESE
BOILER HOUSE
FOOD HALL

Serves 6
EF, DF

Pai-ngapi is a popular pungent seasoning paste used all over Burma but originating from the highland Shan state. Added to everything from stir-fries and soups to curries, it's made from fermented black soy beans and is earthy and garlicky with a touch of sweetness. Soe, the founder of Soe Burmese market stall, wanted to sell Shan-style black bean chicken so he came up with a homemade soy bean paste recipe similar to pai-ngapi but made with ingredients that are readily available in the UK. Fermented black soy beans can be found in Chinese stores.

FOR THE SOY BEAN PASTE:

4 tablespoons fermented black beans
¼ small onion, chopped
2 cloves garlic
1 tablespoon sugar
1 teaspoon salt
1 tablespoon sesame seeds

FOR THE BLACK BEAN CHICKEN:

1kg chicken breast cut into bite-size pieces
2 tablespoons potato starch
4 tablespoons oil
6 cloves garlic, chopped
2 medium onions, finely sliced
1 tablespoon dark soy sauce

Make the soy bean paste the day before you plan on cooking this dish, or at least a few hours in advance. Put the fermented black soy beans into a food processor or blender with the onion, garlic, sugar and salt and add 50ml water. Blend until you have a thick, smoothish paste. Scrape into a bowl and mix in the sesame seeds, then refrigerate for a few hours or preferably overnight to allow the flavours to meld.

When you are ready to make the dish, dust the chicken pieces with the potato starch. Heat the oil in a wok and fry the chicken for four to five minutes on medium-high heat, until golden. Remove the chicken to a plate, then add the garlic and onions to the wok and sauté for three minutes. Stir through the bean paste and return the chicken to the pan. Add the soy sauce and stir fry over medium-high heat for five minutes until the chicken is cooked through and the sauce is unctuous and glossy – if it looks too dry add a splash of water. Serve with rice or noodles.

WHOLE ROASTED BABY CHICKEN
WITH SARLADAISE POTATOES

BLANCHETTE
204 BRICK LANE

Serves 4
GF, WF, EF

In her review of Blanchette East, Fay Maschler likened it to 'a French summer by way of Brick Lane', which pretty much sums up the pleasures of this lovely bistro. Maxime, Malik and Yannis Alary are the brothers behind the restaurant (and its sister restaurant in Soho), and have produced a classic modern Parisian menu that takes in influences from southern France and North Africa. This recipe from executive chef Tam Storror is a favourite from their menu: it does take time but the brining stage rewards you with perfectly tender roast chicken, fragrant with lemon, tarragon and garlic. The sarladaise potatoes are roasted in duck or goose fat, making this a real treat.

FOR THE BRINE:
100g sugar
100g salt

FOR THE CHICKEN:
1 small whole chicken
100g butter
½ lemon
2 garlic cloves, peeled
175ml white wine
500ml good-quality chicken
  stock (Heston's is good)
1 bunch fresh tarragon, chopped

Start off with the brine. Bring 1.6 litres of water to the boil in a big saucepan and add the sugar and salt. Stir until the sugar and salt are completely dissolved, then take off the heat and leave to cool. Remove and discard the wing tips and giblets from the chicken and place it in the brine. Leave for two and half hours in the fridge. Once the brine has done its work, drain the chicken and pat it dry with kitchen paper. Place in a heavy-bottomed roasting dish.

Preheat the oven to 220°C (200°C fan). Melt 50g of the butter in a pan, then pour it over the chicken. Squeeze over the lemon, tuck the garlic cloves into the dish, then pour in the wine and stock. Pop the chicken in the oven and roast for 45 to 60 minutes, or until the juices run clear when you poke a skewer into the thigh.

FOR THE POTATOES:

6 medium-sized potatoes for
   chipping or roasting, peeled
2 garlic cloves, finely chopped
½ bunch fresh rosemary or
   thyme, finely chopped

Keep an eye on the sauce in the tray and don't let it over-reduce –
you can always add a splash of water.

Once the chicken is in the oven, start on the potatoes. Cut them
into 2cm cubes, then parboil in salted water for five minutes.
Drain and let them dry off a bit, then ruffle by gently tossing in the
colander. Melt the duck or goose fat in a roasting tray, then add the
potatoes and shake them around so that they are covered in the
fat. Roast for around 20 minutes, turning regularly, until golden all
over. Add the garlic and rosemary or thyme to the roasted potatoes
when they have reached the desired colour. Return to the oven for
two minutes (keep an eye on the garlic as it may burn).

When the chicken is cooked, leave it to rest for ten minutes or so,
loosely covered in foil. Transfer the stock and juices to a saucepan
and bring to a simmer. Whisk in the remaining 50g of butter and
the fresh tarragon. Serve the chicken with potatoes on the side
and plenty of jus.

PINEAPPLE & NAGA CHILLI GLAZED CHICKEN

Serves 4
DF, EF

My Bengali-inspired twist on the classic roast chicken. Caramelised, sweet and hot, this is great with a variety of sides, British or Bangladeshi. The distinct flavour of the Naga chilli – one of the hottest chillies in the world and native to Bangladesh – is the invisible hero of the marinade. The Naga chilli looks like a skinny version of the scotch bonnet pepper, but is much hotter and has the most amazing fragrance. I add just enough chilli to know it's there – hence the eighth specified in the recipe. You don't need to worry about the marinade being too hot as it covers a good amount of chicken and the sugar and syrupy pineapple also help to tone down the heat. You're left with perfect fall-off-the-bone chicken with a gentle kick.

8 chicken thighs, skinned
  but left on the bone
¼ small onion, chopped
3cm fresh ginger, sliced
⅛ red pepper, roughly chopped
100g tinned pineapple in syrup,
  drained
⅛ Naga chilli
2 tablespoons distilled white
  vinegar
2 tablespoons brown sugar
1½ teaspoons salt
¼ teaspoon pepper
½ teaspoon mixed spice
½ teaspoon nigella seeds

Lightly score each piece of chicken three or four times. This helps it to absorb the flavour of the marinade. Place the chicken pieces in a bowl. Put the chopped onion, ginger, red pepper, pineapple and Naga chilli into a blender. Be very careful when handling the chilli – hold it by the stem to chop or use gloves so you don't make direct contact. Blend until almost smooth but be careful not to overdo it as it will turn into juice. Pour the mixture onto the chicken, then add the vinegar, brown sugar, salt, pepper, mixed spice and nigella seeds. Mix well and set aside for 30 minutes at room temperature, or overnight in the fridge.

Preheat your oven to 220°C (200°C fan) 15 minutes before you're ready to cook your chicken. Roast for 30 to 40 minutes until golden, turning once halfway and then again five minutes before you take the chicken out. Try serving with masala fries (page 146) for an Asian-inspired chicken and chips!

BULGOGI
KOREAN BEEF BARBECUE

SSAMBOP
BOILER HOUSE FOOD
HALL

Serves 4
DF, EF

Bulgogi is the signature dish from Ssambop, the Korean barbecue stall you can find at the market every Sunday. The owner, Kisu, has expert knife skills with which he slices and carves his meat and vegetables, so recreating this at home may not measure up! He barbecues delicate pieces of beef that have been marinated in aromatic spices but you can pan fry them for a similar result (although you won't get any of the smokiness which makes his so special). For rice syrup try a health food store.

500g beef tenderloin fillet steak
1 pear, peeled and
  roughly chopped
½ onion, roughly chopped
4 garlic cloves, finely chopped
2cm fresh ginger, grated
1 spring onion, chopped
2 tablespoons brown sugar
2 tablespoons soy sauce
1 tablespoon rice syrup
1 tablespoon toasted sesame oil
1 carrot, shaved into strips

First slice the beef as finely as possible. Process the chopped pear and onion to a purée and scrape into a bowl. Add the garlic, ginger, spring onion, brown sugar, soy sauce, rice syrup and sesame oil. Add the sliced beef and carrot strips and mix well. Marinate for at least an hour, or preferably overnight in the fridge.

When you're ready to cook, heat up a griddle pan or fire up your barbecue. Cook the beef and carrot pieces on high heat for three to five minutes, depending on how well done you like your meat. Serve with steamed rice and ssamjang – a Korean dipping sauce you can buy online at Sous Chef (www.souschef.co.uk).

SIMPLE XI'AN
BEEF BURGERS

BIANG
STREET FOOD MARKET

Serves 4 as a main,
8 as a snack
DF, EF

Biang founders Fan, Renxiang and Wen described these as the Chinese equivalent of burgers, but I think they're a bit more special than that. An inexpensive cut of meat is stewed in an aromatic broth of Chinese spices until meltingly tender and soft, then stuffed into soft, homemade buns. Fan is keen to stress that this recipe is a simplified version (in case purists are reading!) but the taste is anything but.

FOR THE STEWED BEEF:

500g beef flank
1 teaspoon peppercorns
  (preferably Sichuan)
1 teaspoon fennel seeds
1½ teaspoons chilli flakes
1 star anise
small stick of cinnamon
3cm fresh ginger, sliced
1½ tablespoons soy sauce
1 teaspoon salt
1 teaspoon sesame oil

FOR THE CHINESE BURGER BUNS:

½ teaspoon yeast
½ teaspoon sugar
500g plain flour
oil, to brown each side

Cut the beef into large chunks and place in a saucepan. Add enough water to cover and bring to a boil over high heat. Skim off any foam from the top, then add the peppercorns, fennel seeds, chilli flakes, star anise, cinnamon, ginger, soy sauce, salt and sesame oil to the pot. Reduce the heat to medium-low, cover with a lid and leave it to stew for an hour and half, stirring occasionally. The stew is done when the meat is soft enough to cut with a fork, and the broth is slightly reduced and aromatic.

To make a simplified Chinese bun, add yeast and sugar to 100ml warm water and let it sit for about five minutes. Put the flour into a large mixing bowl and add the yeast mixture along with another 200ml water to make a soft dough. Knead lightly, then cover with a damp tea towel and leave to rise for an hour. Once the dough has risen, divide it into eight portions. Roll each into a ball between your palms, pressing to flatten slightly, then roll out on a floured surface into rounds just under a centimetre thick.

At this point preheat your oven to 190°C (170°C fan).

Heat a frying pan with a little oil on medium heat and lightly brown the uncooked buns until both sides are lightly golden. Move to a lined baking sheet – you may need two – and bake for around 20 to 30 minutes, or until the buns have puffed up and turned golden.

To assemble your burgers, slit one side of each bun (like a pitta pocket). Roughly chop the beef and fill the bun, adding a teaspoon of broth from the stockpot (and some fresh chopped coriander if you like). Enjoy. If you're hungry, you'll easily eat two of these.

ARGENTINIAN-STYLE STEAK
WITH CHIMICHURRI SAUCE

TOROPAMPA
SUNDAY
UPMARKET

Serves 4
DF, EF

Husband and wife team Gabriela and Gonzalo run this Argentinian family butchers specialising in steak and chorizo sausages which they sell at markets and from their online store. This steak with chimichurri is one of their market stall signature dishes and epitomises the Argentinian love of grilled meats simply cooked with good seasoning. Gabriela stresses that the key to a good steak is just to use the best quality meat you can buy.

FOR THE CHIMICHURRI SAUCE:

1 bunch parsley, finely chopped
2 garlic cloves, finely chopped
1 tablespoon chopped
  fresh oregano
1 tablespoon finely chopped
  red pepper
100ml light olive oil
100ml cider or distilled
  malt vinegar
½ teaspoon freshly ground
  black pepper
salt, to taste

FOR THE STEAK:

4 ribeye steaks, each weighing
  around 250g
salt
freshly ground black pepper

To prepare the chimichurri, mix the parsley, garlic, oregano and red pepper in a bowl. Add the olive oil, vinegar and black pepper, then stir gently and taste to see if you would like to add salt or adjust any of the other ingredients. The quantity of each ingredient depends a lot on the taste of the cook and will be different in every Argentinian kitchen!

Bring the steaks to room temperature and heat your grill to high. Season the steaks with salt and pepper and grill on a baking tray for eight to ten minutes on each side, depending how well done you like them. Spoon about a tablespoon of chimichurri sauce over the steaks a minute before they are done to intensify the flavour, then take them out of the grill and leave to rest for a couple of minutes. Serve with a salad or potatoes and plenty more chimichurri.

MILANESA A LA NAPOLITANA
BREADED STEAK

TOROPAMPA
SUNDAY
UPMARKET

Serves 4

This is another Argentinian favourite from the Toropampa stall, particularly popular in Buenos Aires: Milanese-style breaded meat, topped with tomato sauce, cheese and sometimes ham and popped in the oven until golden. It's a winner.

4 rump steaks
3 small eggs
small handful parsley,
  finely chopped
2 garlic cloves, finely chopped
250g breadcrumbs
50g Parmesan cheese
1 tablespoon oil
1 onion, finely chopped
500g tomato passata
4 slices ham (optional)
4 slices Cheddar cheese
salt
freshly ground black pepper

300ml oil, to shallow fry

Put each steak between pieces of cling film and bash with a rolling pin to a thickness of about 5mm. Set aside.

Beat the eggs in a bowl, then add the parsley, garlic, half a teaspoon of salt and a little black pepper. Mix well. In another bowl mix the breadcrumbs and the Parmesan cheese. Dip a steak into the egg mixture, then press into the cheesy breadcrumbs and coat both sides, pressing with your hands to make sure you fully cover the meat. Repeat until all the steaks are breaded. Now prepare the tomato sauce. Put the tablespoon of oil in a pan on medium heat, then add the onion and cook for two minutes. Add the tomato passata and season with half a teaspoon of salt and some black pepper. Simmer for a couple of minutes, then turn off the heat.

Heat the 300ml of oil in a wide, deep pan on medium-high heat. Gently slide in two steaks at a time and fry for about five minutes on each side or until golden brown. Remove and set aside on kitchen paper to drain while you fry the remaining two steaks. Put the cooked steaks in an oven dish and cover each one with a few tablespoons of tomato sauce. If you're using ham, put a slice on each steak, then top with a slice of cheese. Bake for five minutes until the cheese melts. Serve with salad, potatoes or chips.

BEEF BOURGUIGNON BURGER

THE PATATE
SUNDAY
UPMARKET

Serves 4
EF

Martin and Paul-Henry first met at cookery school in France, only to cross paths again three years later at Camden Market. They decided to dive into the street food business together as The Patate, and came up with their star dish: beef bourguignon burgers. They make a traditional beef bourguignon then give it the Patate treatment; grilling portions to order and serving them, covered in jus, in a toasted potato bun with their special sauce (a trade secret, obviously), lettuce, and a choice of Raclette, Fourme d'Ambert or Applewood smoked Cheddar.

100g butter
4 onions, sliced
5 carrots, sliced
700g chuck beef, cut into
    6cm pieces
2 tablespoons plain flour
1 bottle red wine
1 bouquet garni (or a few bay
    leaves, parsley stalks
    and sprigs of thyme)
salt
black pepper

TO SERVE:
4 toasted potato buns,
    or buns of your choice
4 slices cheese
lettuce

Melt 50g of the butter in a frying pan, then fry the onions and carrots for three or four minutes over medium heat until they start to soften. Transfer them to a casserole dish. Dust the meat with the flour. Melt the remaining butter in another pan, then sear the meat until it is a deep-brown colour all over – about five minutes. Remove the meat from the pan and add it to the casserole dish.

Deglaze the frying pan with some of the red wine and bring to a boil. Season with salt and black pepper and pour into the casserole dish. If you don't have bouquet garni to hand, make your own by wrapping your herbs in a small square of muslin and tying with a piece of string, then throw that in too.

Pour the rest of the wine into the casserole, then simmer uncovered for at least three hours on low heat. When the beef is very tender, discard the bouquet garni and leave to cool to room temperature.

To make your own 'The Patate'-style burger, you can grill some of the pieces of meat and place on a warm potato bun. Pour over a little of the jus, then add a slice of cheese, lettuce and sauce of your choice. Bon appétit!

CHOLENT
JEWISH STEW

BEIGEL SHOP
155 BRICK LANE

Serves 4
DF, EF

Family-run Beigel Shop is the oldest bagel bakery in Britain, one of the last remaining vestiges of a time when Brick Lane was home to a thriving Jewish community. Established in 1855, Beigel Shop is one of two remaining bagel bakeries in the area and is iconic of Brick Lane food culture. When I asked manager Hayley for some classic Jewish dishes she and her family eat at home, she gave me her recipe for this traditional stew. Cholent is cooked overnight on a Friday and eaten for lunch on the Saturday, when Sabbath is observed. It's very easy but it's best to plan for it as you need to leave it in the oven for at least 12 hours. Definitely a comfort food staple.

1 tablespoon vegetable oil

1 medium onion, roughly chopped

750g beef brisket, cut into large chunks

125g pearl barley

750g potatoes, peeled and cut into thirds

50g dry pinto beans, soaked overnight

50g dry kidney beans, soaked overnight

1½ teaspoons garlic powder

½ teaspoon paprika

1 teaspoon salt

½ teaspoon black pepper

First, add the oil to a large oven-safe pot and sauté the onions over medium heat. Add the meat and brown for around five minutes. Rinse and drain the barley and add into the pot along with the potatoes and drained pinto beans. Boil the soaked kidney beans in water over high heat for ten minutes, then drain and add to the pot. Sprinkle in the garlic powder, paprika, salt and black pepper.

Give everything a stir to make sure it is distributed evenly inside the pot and then add enough water to cover the meat and potatoes. Bring to a boil, then lower the heat and simmer, partially covered, for ten minutes. Don't stir as this will break the potatoes. Preheat your oven to 120°C (100°C fan). Cover the pot tightly, and put it on the bottom shelf of the oven. Leave the stew to cook overnight. The next morning, check to see if it needs a bit more water, then put back in the oven until lunchtime.

SALT BEEF

BEIGEL SHOP
155 BRICK LANE

Serves 12
GF, WF, EF, DF

Another classic recipe from this award-winning bagel shop. Bagels are made to order with various fillings and salt beef is easily the favourite one, layered onto a fresh bagel with mustard and pickles, and especially loved by Londoners. This is manager Hayley's recipe: while the saltpetre isn't crucial, the salt beef won't keep as long without it and it won't have the deep pinky red colour of the beef you see in their window. I get my saltpetre online from Surfy's Homecuring Supplies (www.homecuring.co.uk). For an authentic beigel experience, eat your salt beef on a real bagel/beigel from a Jewish bakery – supermarket substitutes just won't do!

FOR THE BRINE:

300g soft light brown sugar

350g coarse sea salt

2 teaspoons black peppercorns

2 teaspoons juniper berries

1 tablespoon coriander seeds

3 bay leaves

3 sprigs thyme

1 tablespoon mustard seeds

50g Prague Powder Number
  One or saltpetre (optional)

1 teaspoon chilli flakes
  (optional)

FOR THE BEEF:

2.5kg piece beef brisket

1 carrot, cut into large chunks

1 leek, cut into chunks

1 celery stick, cut into chunks

1 onion, quartered

6 garlic cloves

handful parsley stalks

In a deep casserole dish or large pan, add all the brine ingredients to three litres of water. Slowly bring to the boil and gently simmer for two or three minutes until the sugar and salt have dissolved. Take off the heat and let the brine cool completely.

Pierce the beef brisket all over with a skewer and put in a plastic tub or large heavy-duty ziplock bag. Cover the meat with the brine, making sure it is completely immersed in the liquid. Leave in a cool place or in the fridge for seven days – if you are using a ziplock bag, turn it every day to make sure the meat cures evenly.

After seven days, rinse the brisket thoroughly and place in a large pan with the carrot, leek, celery, onion, garlic and parsley. Add enough water to just cover the meat and bring to a very gentle simmer. Poach for about two and a half hours, or until tender.

Serve hot with potatoes or leave to cool completely in the broth, then remove and shred or slice thinly for sandwiches. The salt beef, well wrapped, will keep in the fridge for up to a week.

HOME-STYLE LAMB AND POTATO CURRY

Serves 4-6
GF, WF, EF, DF

Brick Lane is known for its curry houses and Bangladeshi eateries, and it's no surprise as the largest Bangladeshi population in the UK lives in the area that surrounds this famous foodie hotspot. This is a classic Bengali curry; it does take a little time but it is worth it. Make sure you get lamb on the bone as it is key to those distinct home-style flavours. Mopped up with some flatbread or rice, this is perfect comfort food and it also makes for an impressive dinner party main with sides such as dhal, sautéed vegetables and pilau rice.

4 garlic cloves

5cm piece ginger,
  roughly chopped

1kg lamb shoulder on the bone,
  cut into 3cm pieces

2 medium onions, sliced

1 bay leaf

1 stick cinnamon

6 peppercorns

4 cardamom pods

4 cloves

1 teaspoon mustard seeds

1 star anise

2 teaspoons salt

5 tablespoons vegetable oil

1 tablespoon ground coriander

2 teaspoons ground turmeric

2 teaspoons ground cumin

2 teaspoons chilli powder

2 teaspoons paprika

1 teaspoon garam masala

1 tomato, chopped

700g medium potatoes,
  peeled and quartered

3-4 whole green chillies

2 tablespoons chopped
  fresh coriander

Use a mortar and pestle to crush the garlic and ginger to a paste and place with the meat in a large saucepan over medium heat. Add the onions, bay, cinnamon, peppercorns, cardamom, cloves, mustard seeds, star anise and salt. When the lamb begins to release its juices, place the lid on and leave to cook on low heat for 30 minutes. By now the onions will have almost disintegrated. Turn up the heat to medium and add the oil, stirring through to coat all the meat.

Next, add the ground coriander, turmeric, cumin, chilli powder, paprika and garam masala and cook for a few minutes, stirring regularly. Mix in the chopped tomato and about 100ml water. Cover and cook on medium heat for ten minutes, checking on it regularly and giving it a stir. Add a dash of water if you feel that the meat is catching, or it's drying out too much.

Stir in the potatoes and chillies and cook for five minutes. Add enough hot water to just cover the meat and potatoes and shake the pan gently to mix instead of stirring – the meat and potato will absorb the spices better.

Bring to the boil and simmer on medium-low with the lid on for 20 minutes or until the potato pieces are soft and tender. Check the seasoning and sprinkle over the chopped coriander just before taking off the heat.

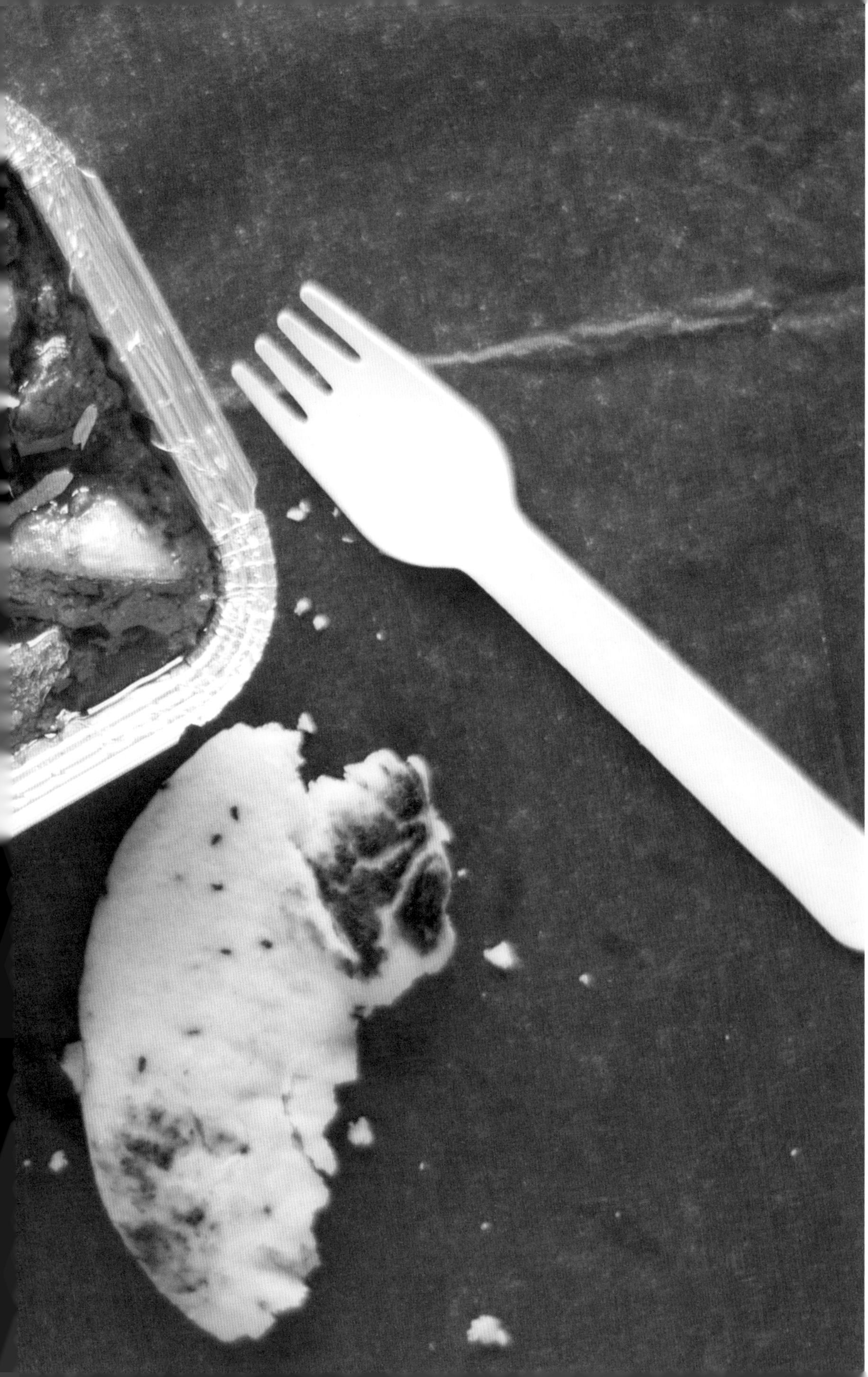

PILAU RICE
WITH PEAS

Serves 4-6
GF, WF, V

This pilau rice is the perfect partner to a curry and only needs about half an hour of cooking time. It's a lovely dish, mildly spiced and fragrant from whole spices, dotted with bright green peas and just as good cold as it is hot. I've used the absorption cooking method which simply uses twice the volume of water to rice.

350g basmati rice

3cm piece ginger,
  roughly chopped

2 tablespoons oil

1 small stick cinnamon

4 cardamom pods

1 bay leaf

1 teaspoon cumin seeds

1 small onion, finely sliced

1 teaspoon salt

⅛ teaspoon ground turmeric

160g frozen peas

Rinse the rice until the water runs clear, then soak for 20 minutes in cold water. Drain the rice and set aside. Crush the ginger with a mortar and pestle. Heat the oil in a saucepan over medium-high heat and add the cinnamon, cardamom, bay leaf and cumin seeds. Stir for 30 seconds to toast the spices, then add the ginger and onion. Add the salt and the turmeric, then sauté for five minutes or so until light golden.

Tip in the rice, stir and gently cook for a couple of minutes, then add 800ml hot water. Bring to the boil on high heat for eight to ten minutes or until small holes appear on the surface of the rice and most of the liquid has been absorbed. Turn the heat to low, scatter the frozen peas over the rice and then cover and cook for 12 to 15 minutes until the pan is letting out steam steadily.

Rest off the heat for at least five minutes and then take the lid off and gently fluff up the rice and mix in the peas with a wooden spoon.

LEMON & CORIANDER RICE

Serves 4-6
V, GF, WF

This rice dish is super simple, fragrant and citrusy. Perfect served hot with a curry or stew, or cold as the base of a bean salad.

▲▲

400g basmati rice, rinsed
1 teaspoon salt
juice and zest of 2 lemons
4 tablespoons chopped
  fresh coriander

Put the rice in a saucepan with a litre of water, then add the salt and bring to the boil on medium-high heat. Boil until most of the water has been absorbed and small holes appear on the surface of the rice. Pour in the lemon juice and zest and gently stir in the coriander, being careful not to break the rice grains. Reduce the heat to low, cover and cook for 12 to 15 minutes, or until a steady stream of steam rises from the pan. Turn off the flame and rest for five minutes before serving. I like this rice with lamb koftas (page 77) or a simple chicken curry.

MUSHROOM, PISTACHIO & PINE NUT RICE

LA BUENAVENTURA
BOILER HOUSE
FOOD HALL

Serves 4
V, WF, GF

Sheila and Herman run the La Buenaventura market stall and specialise in vegan versions of Spanish classics such as chorizo and tapas. This wonderful paella-inspired recipe is wholesome and very tasty, packed full of different flavours and textures. Studded with pistachios and pine nuts, golden with saffron, the finished dish is quite regal looking: add a dollop of La Buenaventura garlic vegannaise (page 172) for a vegan feast.

3 tablespoons olive oil

20g pistachios

30g pine nuts

1 garlic clove, sliced

¼ teaspoon saffron

1½ teaspoons paprika

2 bay leaves

400g mushrooms, sliced

300g paella rice

1 teaspoon turmeric

1 teaspoon salt

Heat the olive oil in a large paella or frying pan over medium heat and fry the pistachios, pine nuts and sliced garlic for a couple of minutes. Add the saffron, paprika, bay leaves and mushrooms and fry for another three to five minutes until the mushrooms have started to soften. Stir in the rice and turmeric, then add a litre of water and the salt. Do not stir the rice while cooking, as this will result in broken rice.

Bring to the boil, then reduce the temperature to a gentle simmer and cook for about 20 minutes, until the rice has absorbed all the liquid.

Remove from the hob and leave the rice to sit for about five minutes. Add a squeeze of lemon before serving.

MASH

SWEET POTATO MASH
WITH CORIANDER & GARLIC

Serves 4
EF, WF, GF

This is my little twist on the classic mashed potato – I love it as a side, but it's equally good as a topping to shepherd's pie. Garlic and coriander add an Asian touch and complement the sweet potato really well. You can replace the milk with your favourite nut milk to make this vegan.

2 medium sweet potatoes,
   peeled and chopped
50ml whole milk
½ teaspoon salt
¼ teaspoon black pepper
1 tablespoon oil
2 garlic cloves, finely grated
2 tablespoons chopped
   fresh coriander

Boil the sweet potato in salted water until soft and tender – about 10 to 12 minutes. Drain and return to the pan and, using a masher, mash the potatoes with the milk until smooth. Season with the salt and pepper and set aside.

In a small frying pan, heat the oil on medium heat and gently fry the garlic until golden. Pour the garlic and oil into the mashed potatoes and place the pan back on the stove on low heat. Mix in the coriander and heat through for a couple of minutes, stirring regularly. Check the seasoning and serve as a side to any fish or meat dish.

POTATO & CARROT MASH

Serves 4
V, GF, WF

This spicy coriander and chilli mash is my go-to dish for when I'm feeling a little under the weather. The potatoes are only slightly mashed, then I stir in some grated carrots at the end of cooking for a bit of texture and freshness. For a classic carb on carb indulgence, this simply has to be eaten with rice or bread. If you're not great with heat, just reduce the chillies by half. The best thing is this dish is served at room temperature so it's great as a sandwich filling and doesn't need to be reheated once cooked.

2 large baking potatoes

2 tablespoons oil

½ medium onion, finely sliced

1½ teaspoons salt

4 green chillies, finely chopped

2 tablespoons chopped
  fresh coriander

1 carrot, grated

Preheat the oven to 200°C (180°C fan). Wash the potatoes and prick all over with a fork. Place on a baking tray and bake for 75 to 90 minutes.

Heat the oil in a frying pan on medium heat and add the onion, salt and chillies. Sauté for a couple of minutes until the onion starts to soften. Turn off the heat.

Scoop the flesh out of the baked potatoes and add to the frying pan along with the coriander. Mix thoroughly with a spoon or a fork, mashing the potato a little, then add the grated carrot. Check the seasoning and adjust if necessary, then serve with plain rice or flatbread.

ROASTED SPICY
BABY POTATOES

Serves 4-6
V, WF, GF

These slightly sweet baby potatoes are roasted with spices, garlic, chilli and a little oil, which makes your kitchen smell even better than when regular roast potatoes are in the oven. I like to serve these with a nice roast. If you happen to have leftovers, have them for brunch. Just smash them up a bit and add to the pan with fried eggs.

1kg baby potatoes

2 tablespoons oil

1 green chilli, finely chopped

2 cloves garlic, grated

2 teaspoons yellow
  mustard seeds

½ teaspoon sea salt

½ teaspoon ground cumin

¼ teaspoon ground turmeric

Preheat the oven to 220°C (200°C fan). Parboil the potatoes in a pan of salted boiling water for about six minutes.

Drain the potatoes and place in a baking dish. Drizzle with the oil, and scatter over the chopped chilli, garlic, mustard seeds, salt, cumin and turmeric. Gently shake the dish to make sure the potatoes are coated evenly with the flavourings, then roast for 30 to 35 minutes, until golden.

MASALA CHIPS
WITH SMOKED PAPRIKA & GARLIC MAYONNAISE

WF, GF

East London is studded with old-fashioned fish and chip shops, and I can barely pass one without being lured in by the comforting hug of frying potatoes. Like most people who've grown up in the UK, not much time goes by before I start to crave this most British of snacks – in my book there's no such thing as too much potato. Here I've jazzed up one of my favourite food items using Desiree potatoes and Asian spices. The chips are boiled first, then fried, keeping them crispy on the outside and soft inside. Chaat masala is crucial to the recipe as it adds a sweet, tangy and sour undertone to the chips: if you're near an Asian grocery store you'll most likely be able to find a packet there. Most major supermarkets tend to store this in their world foods section as well.

FOR THE CHIPS:
1kg Desiree potatoes,
  or another waxy variety

500ml rapeseed oil, to deep fry

FOR THE SMOKED PAPRIKA
& GARLIC MAYONNAISE:
4 tablespoons mayonnaise
2 tablespoons Greek yoghurt
½ teaspoon smoked paprika
1 teaspoon garlic clove,
  finely grated
1 teaspoon oil

Peel and wash the potatoes and slice into 1cm thick slices. Chop each slice lengthways into 1cm wide chips. Place the chipped potatoes into a large bowl of cold water as you go to avoid discolouration. Bring a large pot of salted water to the boil and, when the water is bubbling, carefully slide the drained chips into the pan. Boil for about five minutes, until just tender but still firm. You'll know they're ready when the potato pieces start to lose their opaque appearance.

Drain in a colander and rinse quickly with a burst of cold water. Place in a large plastic ziplock bag and put immediately into the freezer for 20 minutes, being careful not to break the potato pieces.

½ tablespoon chaat masala

½ teaspoon paprika

½ teaspoon dried
  coriander leaves

½ teaspoon chilli flakes

Now make the mayonnaise dip by mixing together the mayonnaise, yoghurt and smoked paprika. Quickly fry the crushed garlic clove in the oil, then stir it into the mayonnaise and put into the fridge.

In a small bowl, mix together the chaat masala, paprika, dried coriander leaves and chilli flakes. Set aside. Heat the rapeseed oil for deep frying in a deep pan on high heat. When the oil is hot, very carefully put half the slightly frozen chips into the pan. Cook for about 15 minutes or until golden, occasionally moving the chips around to get an even colour.

With a slotted spoon transfer the cooked chips to a roasting tin. Sprinkle with about one teaspoon of the masala spice mix and shake the tin so that all the chips are coated with the masala. Repeat for the second batch of chips – if you have a deep fat fryer you can probably fry them in one batch. Devour hot, with the smoked paprika and garlic mayonnaise.

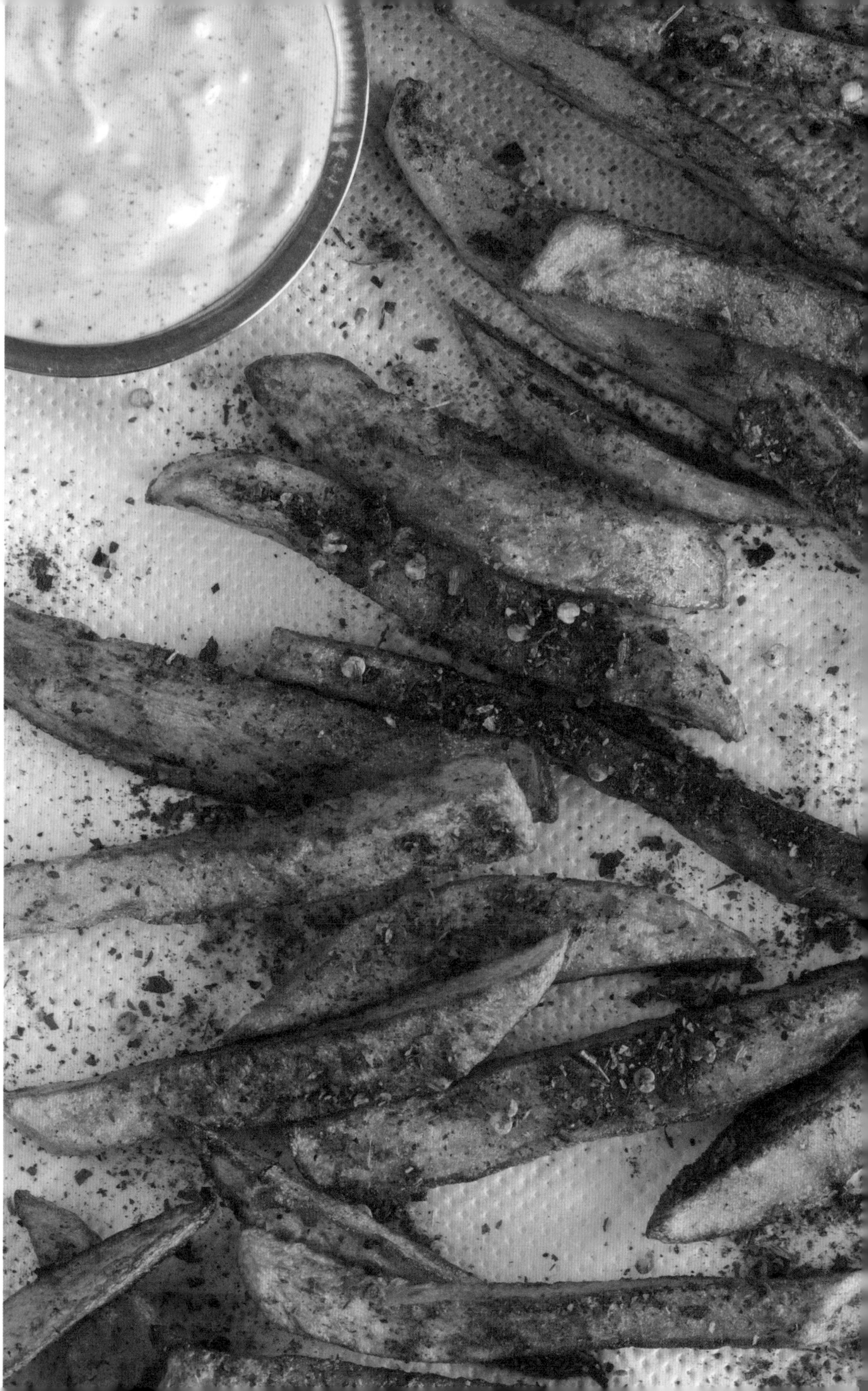

TARKA DHAL

Serves 4-6
V, GF, WF

This simple dhal recipe is a staple in our household and is true Bangladeshi comfort food. It's ready in around half an hour and is light, fragrant and garlicky. So good poured over some steamed basmati rice and of course as a side to a meat or chicken dish. My siblings and I love it mixed into a good lamb and potato curry with everything mashed together.

FOR THE DHAL:

200g red split lentils
½ small onion, finely chopped
½ teaspoon turmeric
1 teaspoon salt
1 bay leaf

FOR THE TEMPERING OR TARKA:

5-6 garlic cloves
2 tablespoons oil
4 dried red chillies
½ teaspoon cumin seeds
1 tablespoon chopped
  fresh coriander

Rinse the red lentils until the water runs clear then put them in a large pot with a litre of water and the onion, turmeric, salt and bay leaf. Bring to the boil and reduce heat to medium-low. Partially cover and simmer for 30 minutes, giving the dhal a stir every ten minutes or so.

When the lentils have almost disintegrated and formed a thick soup-like consistency, prepare the tempering or tarka. Crush the garlic in a mortar and pestle. Heat the oil in a small frying pan on medium heat and add the dried red chillies. Fry until deep brown and then add the crushed garlic and cumin seeds.

Stir lightly until the garlic has turned deep golden and carefully pour the contents of the pan – including the oil – into the pot with the dhal. Give everything a quick stir and add the chopped coriander. Cover and simmer for another couple of minutes and serve with basmati rice.

KERELA & ALOO BHAJI
BITTER GOURD & POTATO CURRY

GRAM BANGLA
68 BRICK LANE

Serves 4
V, GF, WF

This small, unpretentious, café-style Bangladeshi restaurant is owned by Abdul Shahid and is the place for the home-style food missed by many expats. Of all the curry houses that Brick Lane is famous for, Gram Bangla is the place Bengalis go to eat and its simple appeal has caught on in the wider community. Have a look at the open kitchen before ordering a few of the mouth-wateringly authentic dishes displayed opposite the stove where they are cooked. The changing daily menu includes a few staples, such as this vegetable dish which is slightly bitter but super tasty. The chef tells me this is one of the recipes his mother taught him and is a popular side dish in his home region of Sylhet, Bangladesh.

1 medium potato, peeled and chopped into 1cm cubes
3 large bitter gourds
4 tablespoons oil
1 medium onion, finely sliced
1 garlic clove, chopped
1 teaspoon salt
1 teaspoon curry powder
½ teaspoon ground turmeric
½ teaspoon ground cumin
2 green chillies, sliced
2 tablespoons chopped fresh coriander

Rinse the potato pieces and put in a bowl of cold water. Rinse the bitter gourds then top and tail each one. Cut in half lengthways, then across into thin slices. Set aside.

Heat the oil in a frying pan over medium heat and add the sliced onion, garlic and salt. Sauté for three or four minutes until golden. When the onions are golden add the curry powder, turmeric and cumin and stir through for a minute, then add the bitter gourd slices and drained potatoes. Turn up the heat to high and cook, stirring, for a couple of minutes until the gourd has started to wilt. Cover the pan, reduce the heat to medium-low and cook for ten minutes, then add the sliced chillies and cook for a further five minutes or until the potato pieces are tender and break easily when pushed with a fork. Sprinkle with the coriander just before taking off the heat and stir through. Serve with plain rice or flatbread.

Kenyan

Class 1

Gourds (Karella)

100g (Raw) typical value 9 Calories

299p   1kg
2.2lb

SAUTÉED FINE BEANS

Serves 4
V, GF, WF

Brick Lane is famous for its curry houses, but what you won't find on many of the menus are the simple vegetable dishes cooked in every Bangladeshi home. This super simple and quick recipe is a perfect accompaniment for roasted meats or baked fish. Or, if you're cooking up a curry feast, it adds a perfect freshness (obviously with a kick!) to the meal.

350g fine beans
1 tablespoon oil
1 teaspoon panch phoron
1 garlic clove, chopped
1 green chilli, chopped
¼ teaspoon salt
¼ teaspoon ground cumin
¼ teaspoon ground turmeric

Top and tail the beans and blanch in boiling water for three minutes. Drain.

In a separate pan, heat the oil on medium-high heat and add the panch phoron. When the seeds start to pop add the garlic, chilli and salt and cook for 30 seconds. When the garlic has turned golden, stir in the cumin and turmeric. Add the blanched beans, cover and cook for a couple of minutes on medium heat. The beans should be slightly tender but still crunchy. Serve hot.

RICE FLOUR
FLATBREADS

Serves 4
V, WF, GF

A classic Bengali flatbread made with rice flour instead of wheat flour – great if you want to avoid gluten, and delicious enjoyed warm with a light meat curry or your favourite vegetable dish. The recipe calls for equal volumes of water and rice flour so use either a mug or a standard cup to measure them out.

¼ teaspoon salt
1 cup rice flour, plus more
  for rolling

In a pan bring a cup of water to the boil with the salt. Reduce the heat to low, then carefully pour in the flour. Mix thoroughly with a wooden spoon so that everything is well combined and turn the heat to very low. Cover with a lid and let the dough steam for five minutes. Take off the heat and cool for several minutes with the lid partially open, until cool enough to handle. Make sure it doesn't cool too much; otherwise it will be difficult to knead and the finished flatbreads will break up when cooking. Scrape the dough into a bowl and knead for about five minutes until it firms up and holds together into a smooth ball. Cover with a damp cloth and rest for about ten minutes. Again, don't let the mixture cool completely; otherwise the flatbreads will break and won't hold together. Knead for another minute or so and divide into eight equal portions. Roll each one into a ball.

Heat a flat griddle pan or heavy-based frying pan on medium-low heat. A cast iron pan such as an Indian *tawa* works best if you have one. While the pan heats up, generously dust a surface with rice flour and, using a very light touch, roll out each ball into a disc about 1.5 cm thick. Carefully slide a flatbread onto the hot pan and cook for about a minute, then flip it over using a spatula. Cook for another minute and turn over a second time, gently pressing with your spatula around the edges to ensure even cooking. Continue cooking in this way until lightly golden bubbles appear on the surface of each side and serve hot.

SALADS
& SAUCES
SALADS
& SAUCES
SALADS

BEETROOT, SWEETCORN & CARROT SALAD
WITH CORIANDER

Serves 4
V, WF, GF

Sweet, fresh and zingy perfectly describes this salad, which includes two of the best root vegetables and a generous portion of sweetcorn. The citrusy dressing makes this a perfect partner to salmon or chicken.

2 cooked beetroot, grated

2 carrots, grated

1 x 198g tin sweetcorn, drained and rinsed

1 tablespoon fresh lime juice

1 tablespoon olive oil

salt

black pepper

2 tablespoons chopped fresh coriander

Put the beetroot, carrots and sweetcorn in a bowl. Whisk together the lime juice and oil in another small bowl and season with salt and pepper to taste. Pour over the salad, add the chopped coriander and gently but quickly toss everything together. Serve immediately, before the beetroot stains everything purple!

SWEET POTATO, LIME YOGHURT & TOASTED BARLEY SALAD

CAFÉ 1001
91 BRICK LANE

Serves 4
EF, WF

Café 1001 is a vibrant café, lounge and event space situated halfway up Brick Lane and a perfect spot to relax and unwind. They regularly host live music acts, art exhibitions and film screenings and are a big part of the local arts community that makes Brick Lane so special. There's a huge selection of snacks including plenty of vegetarian and vegan options, salads and cakes. Juliana, the head chef, is always creating new, interesting and healthy salads and shared a few of her favourite dishes with me. This sweet potato salad has a wonderful fresh and zingy yoghurt dressing, with extra flavour and bite from the guest ingredient, pearl barley. Delicious!

50g pearl barley
1 large sweet potato
1 tablespoon olive oil
½ teaspoon cumin seeds

FOR THE DRESSING:
200ml yoghurt
juice and zest of 1 lime
2 tablespoons olive oil
1 small garlic clove, crushed
salt
black pepper

TO SERVE:
2–3 spring onions, chopped
1 tablespoon chopped
  fresh coriander

Preheat your oven to 190°C (170°C fan). Place the pearl barley on a baking tray and roast for 20 to 25 minutes. Wash the unpeeled sweet potato and slice into rounds about half a centimetre thick. Toss with the olive oil and cumin seeds, put on another baking tray and roast for 15 minutes or until soft but still firm enough that they won't break up in the salad. Boil the toasted pearl barley in salted water for eight to ten minutes on high heat until tender, being careful not to overcook. Drain thoroughly and set aside.

Make the dressing by mixing the yoghurt with the lime zest and juice, olive oil and crushed garlic in a small bowl. Season to taste with salt and black pepper. To assemble the salad, arrange the roasted sweet potato, pearl barley and spring onions on a platter. Drizzle with the dressing and finish with the chopped coriander for a pop of colour.

TOASTED CAULIFLOWER
WITH A POMEGRANATE DRESSING

CAFÉ 1001
91 BRICK LANE

Serves 4-6
V

There's a whole host of flavours and textures here, which makes it great as a standalone main or as part of a sharing platter. Cauliflower florets are roasted until just browned but still crunchy, then tossed in a sweet yet tart and punchy dressing. It's a real show stopper but does require a little prepping, so give yourself time to enjoy making it.

FOR THE DRESSING:

2½ tablespoons pomegranate
  molasses
1 teaspoon red wine vinegar
¼ garlic clove, crushed
¼ teaspoon Dijon mustard
¼ teaspoon sugar
⅛ teaspoon salt
110ml olive oil
squeeze of lemon juice

FOR THE SALAD:

1 pomegranate
100g hazelnuts
1 large cauliflower
1 tablespoon olive oil
½ stick of celery, chopped into
  1cm cubes
3 tablespoons chopped
  fresh parsley
salt
black pepper

To make the dressing, whisk together the pomegranate molasses, vinegar, garlic, mustard, sugar and salt. Still whisking, slowly add the oil to create an emulsion. Mix in a squeeze of lemon juice and set aside. Peel the pomegranate and pluck out the jewel-like seeds. Put them in a bowl and pick off any pith.

Preheat your oven to 180°C (160°C fan). Place the hazelnuts on a tray and roast for seven minutes. Remove and leave to cool a bit before rolling them with your palms to remove the papery skin. Lightly crush the nuts with the flat of a knife or roughly chop. Increase the oven temperature to 220°C (200°C fan). Break the cauliflower into florets, setting aside the stalks. Toss the florets in the olive oil, season with salt and black pepper and put on a baking tray. Bake for five minutes or until golden brown. Grate the reserved cauliflower stalks.

Combine the roasted cauliflower with the pomegranate seeds, crushed hazelnuts, grated cauliflower stalks and chopped celery. Toss with the dressing and chopped parsley and serve.

TABBOULEH

This super easy, fresh-tasting, Middle-Eastern salad tastes delicious with just about anything and is another regular on the Damascu Bite menu. For a perfect tabbouleh make sure that you chop all the ingredients very finely, especially the parsley, and serve at room temperature. The chef recommends that you be generous with the olive oil and lemon juice as this really helps soften the bulgar wheat and intensify the flavours. Eat with grilled meats, hummus and pitta bread for a delicious Syrian feast.

1 bunch fresh parsley,
   stalks discarded
4 large tomatoes
200ml olive oil
juice of 1½ lemons
5 tablespoons fine brown
   bulgar wheat
small handful fresh mint,
   stalks discarded
salt, to taste

Chop the parsley leaves very finely and put in a mixing bowl. Finely chop the onions and tomatoes and add to the parsley.

Pour in the olive oil and lemon juice and add the bulgar wheat and the chopped mint. Toss everything together, then season to taste with some salt. Allow to sit for about five minutes so that the fine bulgar wheat absorbs the juices from the salad, then serve.

TOMATO, CUCUMBER & RED ONION SALAD

Serves 4-6
V, GF, WF

Variations of this salad are served on small metal plates with your meal in all the Bangladeshi cafés of Brick Lane. Eat it with kebabs, roasted meats and curries, as it pairs perfectly with anything spicy. Mix everything just before serving, to prevent wilting.

1 medium red onion, halved and finely sliced

¼ teaspoon salt

½ medium cucumber, julienned

2 tomatoes, halved and finely sliced

juice of ½ lemon

2 green chillies, finely chopped

4 tablespoons chopped fresh coriander

1 teaspoon mint sauce

Place the onion in a bowl, add the salt and mix well with a wooden spoon or by hand. Set aside while you prep the other ingredients. Add the cucumber, tomato, lemon juice and chilli and combine. Just before serving, mix in the chopped coriander and mint sauce.

BURMESE SOUR
MANGO SALAD

SOE BURMESE
BOILER HOUSE FOOD
HALL

A spicy, sour and hot salad from the guys at the Soe Burmese stall, and the perfect side to their Shan-style black bean chicken (page 112).

Serves 4-6
GF, WF, DF, EF

1 tablespoon vegetable oil

2 cloves garlic, sliced

pinch of turmeric

pinch of salt

1 teaspoon fish sauce

1 teaspoon chilli flakes

1 tablespoon ground
   dried shrimp

1 large green mango, peeled
   and julienned

First make the garlic and chilli dressing. Heat the oil in a pan and lightly fry the garlic until golden. Add a pinch of turmeric and a pinch of salt. Stir for 30 seconds and take the pan off the heat, then add the fish sauce, chilli flakes and ground shrimp. Leave to cool.

Mix the dressing in with the mango and serve.

FRUIT SALAD
WITH CHAAT MASALA

Serves 4-6
V, WF, GF

This Indian-style fruit salad is inspired by the street food I've eaten at the Brick Lane Boishaki Mela, the second largest street festival in the UK after the Notting Hill Carnival. Boishaki Mela marks the beginning of the Bengali New Year (Boishak) which is celebrated in both Bangladesh and West Bengal and is the largest of its kind outside Bangladesh. This springtime tradition includes music, dance, processions and of course street food! This fruit salad is light and refreshing with a little kick from the spices. At festivals they chop up the fruit and mix it up in front of you. The best thing about making it yourself is that you can use a selection of fruits and berries, whatever you have available really – just make sure you have a mixture of sweet and tart fruits which are fresh and seasonal. Chaat masala is a smoky spice blend, which includes black salt and dried mango powder, or *amchur*.

1 Braeburn apple

1 orange

1 medium ripe mango

6 strawberries

1 banana

1 pear

1 teaspoon chaat masala

½ teaspoon chilli flakes

¼ teaspoon chilli powder

¼ teaspoon sea salt

¼ teaspoon black pepper

Chop all the fruit into small, roughly even-sized pieces, then place everything into a bowl. Sprinkle over the chaat masala, chilli flakes and powder, salt and black pepper; mix well and serve immediately.

CUCUMBER RAITA

A super simple recipe for this classic Asian accompaniment. Raita goes perfectly with curries and koftas, or simply dip into it with warm pitta bread for a tasty snack. You can make this with or without the chillies, but I like my raita to have some heat.

¼ cucumber, peeled and
  finely chopped
½ small onion, finely chopped
2 green chillies, finely chopped
250g Greek yoghurt
⅛ teaspoon salt
1 tablespoon chopped
  fresh coriander

The only prep here is the chopping! Mix the cucumber, onion and chillies together with the yoghurt and salt. Stir in the coriander and you're done. This can be made a day ahead and refrigerated until you need it.

VEGANAISSE

LA BUENAVENTURA
BOILER HOUSE FOOD
HALL

Makes about 100ml
V, GF, WF

This simple mayonnaise-alternative is just as delicious as a classic garlic mayonnaise but completely egg free. Serve it with any rice dish or as a dipping sauce – La Buenaventura serve it with their mushroom, pistachio and pine nut rice (page 141). It does have a tendency to split, so make sure you add the sunflower oil very slowly and stop adding it as soon as the mixture emulsifies.

3 garlic cloves
50ml soy milk
1 teaspoon lemon juice
125ml sunflower oil
salt, to taste

Put the garlic cloves and soy milk in the blender cup and mix with your hand blender until creamy. Add the lemon juice and salt to taste and continue blending. Very slowly add the sunflower oil as you keep the blender running – you really need to keep an eye on things as you're doing this. As soon as the veganaisse comes together and emulsifies, turn off the blender and stop adding the oil – you may not need it all.

CRIOLLA SAUCE

MOO CANTINA
62 BRICK LANE

Serves 4
V, WF, GF

Criolla sauce is a classic accompaniment to Argentinian asado or barbecue. Carmen from Moo Cantina described it as a salad and sauce in one, similar to the widely known chimichurri, but even fresher.

2 tomatoes, chopped
1 red pepper, finely chopped
1 small onion, finely chopped
1 garlic clove, crushed
2 tablespoons chopped flat
  leaf parsley
100ml olive oil
50ml red wine vinegar
salt
black pepper

There isn't much to making this apart from the actual prep. Simply place everything together in a mixing bowl and toss together. Enjoy with your grilled or barbecued meats or with Moo Cantina's beef empanadas on page 70.

SWEET
THINGS
SWEET
THINGS

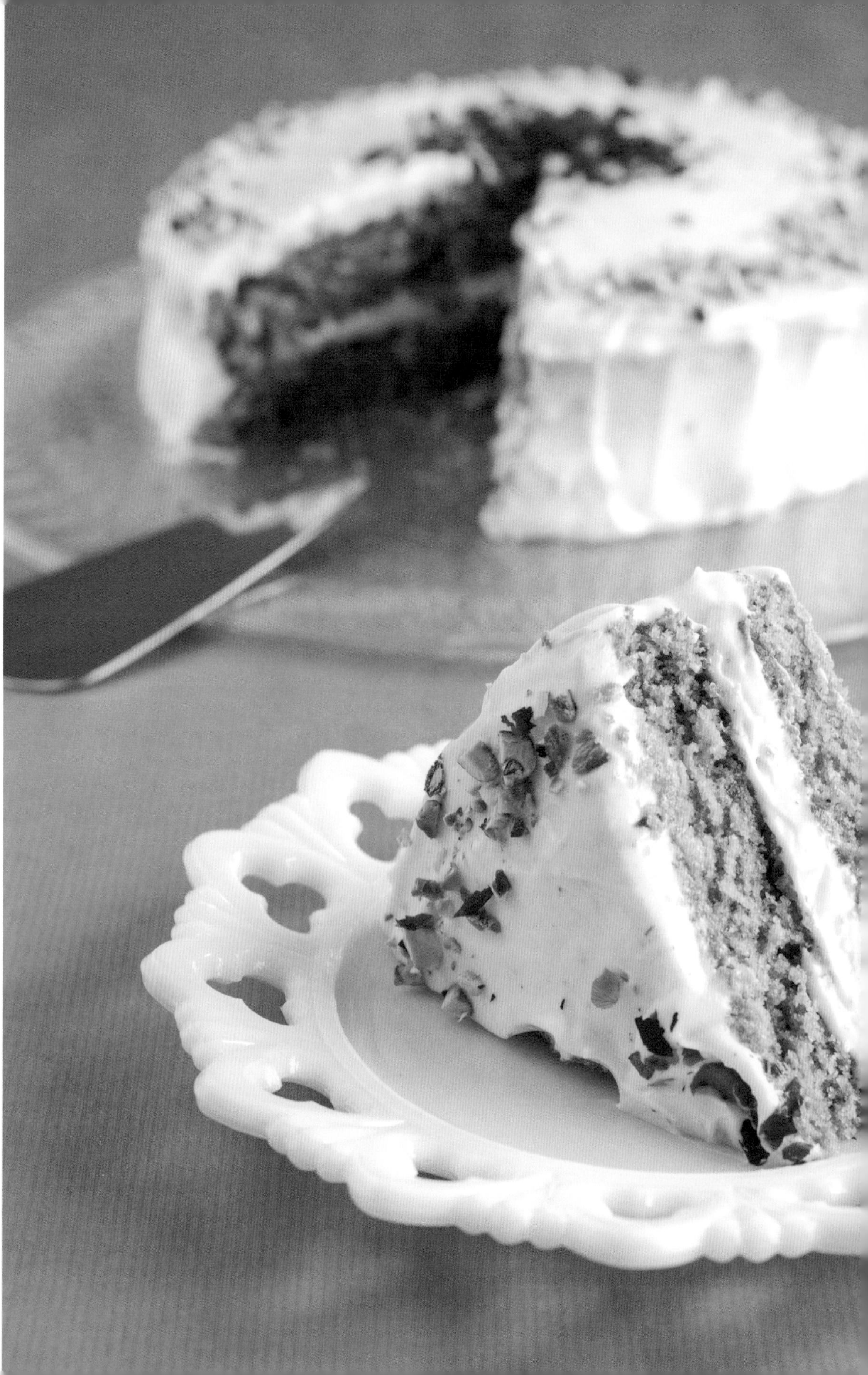

CHAI MALAI CAKE

Serves 10-12

I've seen people's eyes light up after a single bite of this cake and even those who don't normally eat cake are usually converted. Of everything I cook, this is the thing most requested by family and friends. I first created it for a Bengali-inspired afternoon tea and wanted to share the recipe for this book as it's such a wonderful way of showcasing spices in a dessert. The cake layers are reminiscent of fragrant masala chai and the frosting is inspired by rasmalai, the famous Bengali milk-based sweet, flavoured with rosewater and cardamom. Make it as an extra-special birthday cake, decorated with vibrant pink rose petals and pistachios, or as a perfect finish to your next dinner party. For best results, you need a handheld electric mixer or a stand mixer to make the cake, but you can do it with a whisk and some elbow grease.

FOR THE CAKE:

2 tea bags
½ teaspoon ground cardamom
100ml whole milk
½ teaspoon distilled
   white vinegar
175g unsalted butter,
   at room temperature
200g caster sugar
1 teaspoon vanilla extract
1 teaspoon ground cinnamon
1 teaspoon ground ginger
2 tablespoons Greek yoghurt
225g self-raising flour

Preheat your oven to 180°C (160°C fan) and grease and line the cake tins.

Steep the tea bags in 100ml boiling water, stirring for a minute to extract as much of the flavour as possible. Discard the teabags. Add the ground cardamom to the tea and stir thoroughly, then set aside to let it infuse – this gives you a really fragrant batter. Make your buttermilk next: pour the milk into a glass and stir in the vinegar. Let this sit while you start on the cake batter.

In a large bowl, cream together the butter, sugar and vanilla with a handheld mixer until light and fluffy – this will take at least two minutes. If you're using a non-electric whisk you'll need to beat the mixture for longer.

Cont...

1½ teaspoons baking powder

¼ teaspoon salt

3 medium egg whites

FOR THE FROSTING:

100g unsalted butter, at room
   temperature

½ teaspoon ground cardamom

180g full-fat cream cheese

½ teaspoon vanilla extract

2 tablespoons rosewater

250g icing sugar

TO DECORATE:

1 tablespoon dried rose petals

1 tablespoon crushed pistachios

2 x 20cm springform cake tins

Add the cinnamon, ginger and yoghurt and beat for a further minute, then slowly beat in the tea and buttermilk

Put the flour in a separate bowl with the baking powder and salt and quickly mix with a whisk. Add the flour to the buttermilk, butter and sugar mixture in two or three additions, then whisk for about 30 seconds until everything is well combined. Make sure not to overmix at this point or you'll lose the lightness in the cake.

Put the egg whites into a clean mixing bowl. Beat with a clean whisk until they form stiff peaks – five minutes or so (longer, if non-electric). Gently fold the egg whites into the cake batter until evenly combined and pour it into the prepared tins. Bake for 25 to 30 minutes, or until a toothpick poked into the middle comes out clean. Cool completely in the tins on a wire rack.

When you are ready to make the frosting, beat the butter with the ground cardamom until pale and fluffy. Mix in the cream cheese, vanilla extract and rosewater, then slowly add the icing sugar and whisk together until you have a smooth, glossy frosting.

Put one of the cake layers on a large, pretty plate. Using a palette knife, spread with a third of the frosting, then turn the second cake layer upside down and place on top, very gently pressing together to sandwich. Then take the remaining frosting and pile it on top of the second layer. Gently coax some of the frosting down to cover the sides, turning as you go, and smooth the rest in a good thick layer over the top.

Finish the cake with two concentric circles of vibrant pink dried rose petals and crushed pistachios and dot a couple of rose petals in the centre. This cake is a stunner! It tastes best after resting in the fridge for a couple of hours, as this helps the flavours meld together and makes the cake easier to cut.

Cook's tip – you can bake the cake layers in advance. Just completely cool, wrap in cling film and put in the fridge overnight. The cake will stay fresh and moist.

PISTACHIO CAKES
WITH A JAMMY GLAZE

Makes 12

These cakes are inspired by the pretty cake displays in the window of Kahaila café, which always grab my attention. The subtle taste of pistachios mixes perfectly with buttery sponge and a jammy glaze. It's amazing how simply peeling the cases off these cupcakes and topping them with a little icing and a vibrant sprinkle of pistachios can make them look so dainty!

FOR THE CAKES:

120g butter, softened

120g caster sugar

2 medium eggs

50ml milk

¼ teaspoon salt

½ teaspoon vanilla extract

½ teaspoon baking powder

120g self-raising flour

60g pistachios

FOR THE GLAZE:

2–3 tablespoons apricot jam

50g icing sugar

12 hole muffin tin

Preheat your oven to 180°C (160°C fan) and line a 12 hole muffin tin with cupcake cases.

First add your pistachios to a grinder and blitz until finely ground. Set aside, reserving a tablespoonful to decorate the cakes. Cream the butter and sugar together in a mixing bowl and whisk in the eggs, milk, salt and vanilla extract. Add the baking powder to the flour and then mix into the wet ingredients in two or three batches until the mixture is smooth. Fold in the ground pistachios. Divide the batter between the cupcake cases and bake for 12 to 15 minutes until risen and golden.

Let the cakes cool slightly in the tin, then peel off their cases and, while they're still warm, brush the top of each one with a little warmed apricot jam. Put the icing sugar in a small bowl and add a teaspoon of cold water. You want quite a thick icing, but if it's too thick add a drop more water. Make a little cone from a 15cm square of greaseproof paper, and fold the tip. Fill with the icing, then unfold the tip and cut the very end off it to make a thin nozzle. Pipe four or five diagonal lines on each cake, and finish off with a sprinkle of the reserved ground pistachios.

LEMON, EARL GREY & ALMOND FRIANDS

KAHAILA CAFÉ
135 BRICK LANE

Makes 12

Kahaila's flagship Brick Lane café opened in 2012 and is a not-for-profit community café, which supports local community projects and other charitable causes. In my opinion it's one of the nicest coffee shops on Brick Lane and it provides a great urban space for meetings, collaborations and relaxing. Stunning cakes and baked goods are sourced ethically and locally and line the window display, luring cake fiends inside. These elegant little friands are made by Luminary Bakery and are wonderfully fragrant with the addition of my favourite tea – Earl Grey – to the almond frangipane batter. Perfect with a cup of Earl Grey and a slice of lemon.

FOR THE CAKES:

150g unsalted butter, softened

150g white caster sugar

2 medium eggs

zest of 1 lemon

200g ground almonds

40g plain flour

leaves from 2 Earl Grey tea bags

30g flaked almonds

FOR THE GLAZE:

2 tablespoons shredless
   marmalade

3 tablespoons lemon curd,
   plus more for piping

1 tablespoon Earl Grey
   tea leaves

12 hole muffin tin

Preheat your oven to 180°C (160°C fan). Grease the holes of your muffin tin and dust with flour, shaking it to make sure they've got an even coating.

In a large bowl, cream the butter and sugar with an electric mixer until pale and fluffy. Beat in the eggs, one at a time, followed by the lemon zest, ground almonds, plain flour and tea leaves. Divide the frangipane batter equally between the muffin holes, smoothing out the tops with the back of a teaspoon. Sprinkle a few flaked almonds across the top of each one and bake in the oven for about 15 to 20 minutes.

When the cakes are cooked they'll be golden brown around the edges and will spring back slightly to the touch (if you undercook these you'll struggle to get them out the tins). Remove the cakes from the oven and allow them to cool a little in the tin before turning them out onto a wire rack. You may need to carefully run a knife around the edge of each cake if they're a little stuck.

When the cakes are cold, make the glaze. Mix the marmalade and lemon curd with a few drops of water. Add the tea leaves and warm through in the microwave until really runny and bubbling – around 20 seconds. Carefully brush the hot glaze over the top of each cake with a pastry brush so they're super shiny. Pipe a small circular blob of lemon curd off-centre on top of each cake. Sprinkle some Earl Grey tea leaves in a thin asymmetrical straight line across the lemon curd blob.

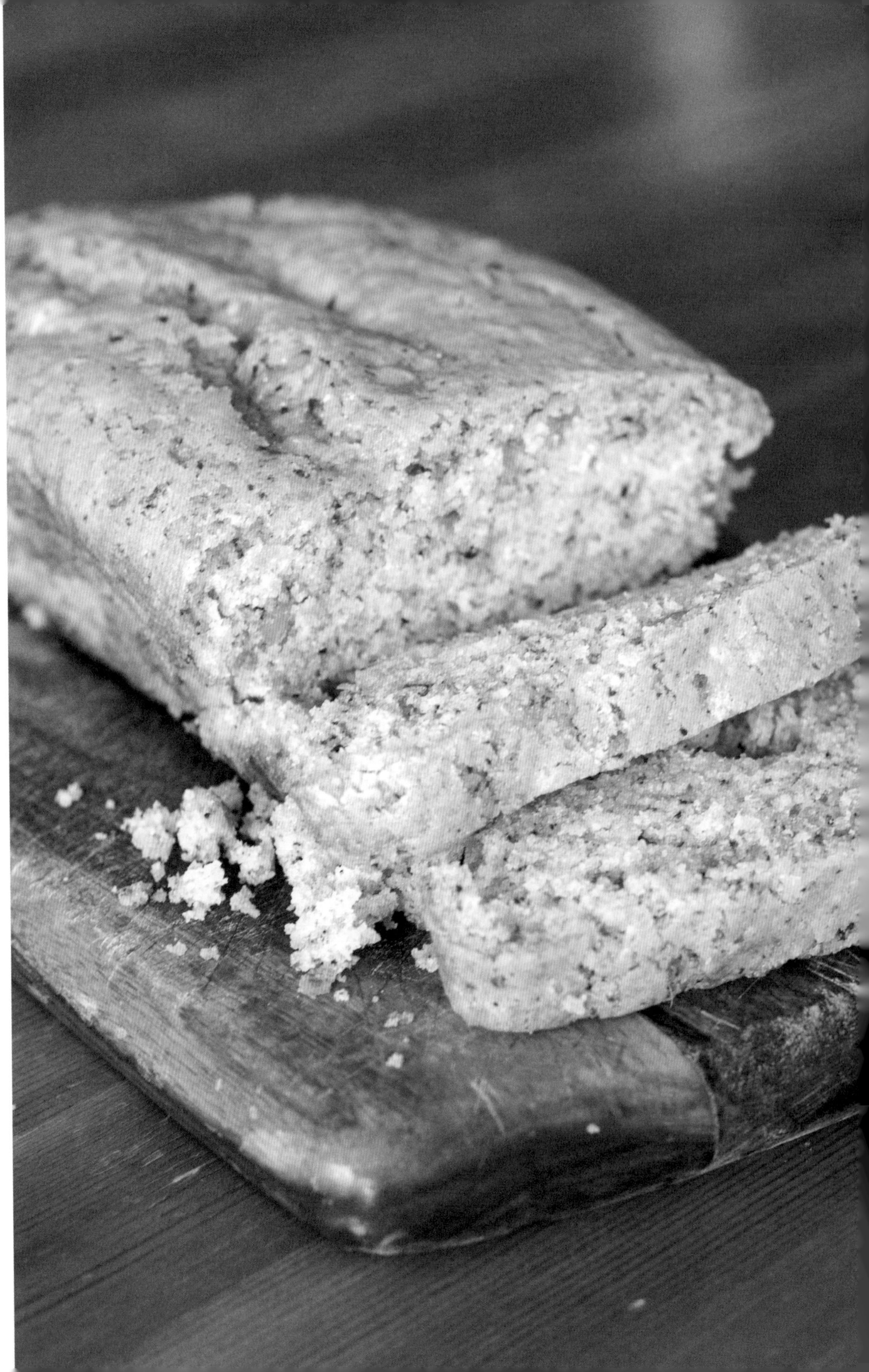

SUPER EASY YOGURT CAKE

LA BUENAVENTURA
BOILER HOUSE
FOOD HALL

Serves 6
V

I first heard of Sheila Latorre and Hernan Piño, the husband and wife team behind La Buenaventura, when we were both trading at Walthamstow Village market in 2016, but I had never met them. I'd heard great things about their 100% plant-based Spanish food though, so I was delighted to find out that they also traded at Brick Lane every Sunday and even more pleased when they gave me some recipes. This vegan cake is really versatile and you can easily make your own variations. Measurements are all based on a small 125g yogurt pot – you can use any flavoured yogurt, or use plain and add some lemon juice and lemon zest. Try stirring some nuts and dried fruits into the batter, or substituting a little of the flour for cocoa powder for a chocolatey cake – the possibilities are endless!

3 tablespoons ground flaxseed
125g pot soy or coconut yogurt
1 pot sunflower oil
2 pots sugar
3 pots plain flour
1 tablespoon baking powder

23 x 13cm loaf tin

Preheat your oven to 180°C (160°C fan).

Mix the ground flaxseed with nine tablespoons of water and set aside for a few minutes. Put the yoghurt in a large bowl, then using the empty pot as a measure, add the sunflower oil. Stir in the flaxseed mix and blend with a stick blender. Add the sugar, plain flour and baking powder and blend until you have a smooth batter. If the mix is too thick you can add a bit of soy milk.

Oil your cake tin thoroughly and pour the batter. Bake for 45 minutes or until a knife or toothpick poked into the middle of the cake comes out dry. Cool on a wire rack before slicing.

BROWN BUTTER, ALMOND & ROSE MINI BUNDTS

Makes 12

I first discovered brown butter on holiday in France when I made it to add to a cake. I was so delighted with the results that I rushed to show my friend excitedly. 'Look! Butter has almost turned into caramel!' Who knew such alchemy? Back in London I decided to experiment further with brown butter, adding it to biscuits and tart shells – I was convinced browning butter was absolutely the best way to eat it. I decided to make mini bundt cakes using my mum's old tin and, of course, brown butter had to feature in the recipe. The colour of these little cakes reminded me of the golden flakes of baklava pastry, so I've added a Middle Eastern twist with a rose-scented icing. One of these is never enough so double up the recipe if you're a greedy sort like me.

FOR THE CAKES:

100g unsalted butter

100g caster sugar

¼ teaspoon salt

40g ground almonds

½ teaspoon vanilla extract

¼ teaspoon almond extract

2 medium eggs

110g self-raising flour

2 tablespoons milk

Place the butter in a stainless steel pan on medium heat (you need to be able to monitor the colour of the butter so you don't burn it). The butter will begin to foam after about 30 seconds. Cook for a further three or four minutes until it starts to smell nutty, almost caramel-like. You will begin to see small particles of milk solid at the bottom on the pan. Once done, take the pan off the heat and leave to cool for about ten minutes. Now preheat the oven to 180°C (160°C fan). Generously grease your bundt tins, dust with flour and shake off the excess.

FOR THE ROSE ICING & TOPPING:

100g icing sugar

2 drops pink food colouring
  (optional)

2–3 tablespoons milk

2 teaspoons rosewater

50g flaked almonds, toasted

12 ring mini bundt tin

When the butter has cooled, transfer to a mixing bowl and cream together with the sugar, salt, ground almonds and vanilla and almond extracts. Whisk the eggs in a small bowl, then beat them into the butter and sugar mixture. Pour in half the flour and mix thoroughly, then add the milk and remaining flour. Mix until you have a smooth, thick batter.

Divide the batter between the bundt rings, filling them to about a centimetre from the top. Bake for 15 to 18 minutes or until lightly risen and pale gold. If you're anything like me you'll find the scent of freshly baked cake irresistible and will want to dig right in but don't, unless you want broken halves of warm sponge in your hand! Let the cakes cool completely in the tin for about an hour, then run a thin butter knife around the edge of each cake and ease them out.

Place the cakes on a baking rack or a flat dish and prepare the icing. Put the icing sugar in a small bowl and add the pink food colouring, two tablespoons of milk and the rosewater. Mix together to make a pretty pink icing, runny enough to drizzle – if it looks too thick add another tablespoon of milk. Top each cake with a teaspoon or so of the icing, gently coaxing drips down the sides. Top with some flaked almonds and serve with a fragrant cup of masala tea.

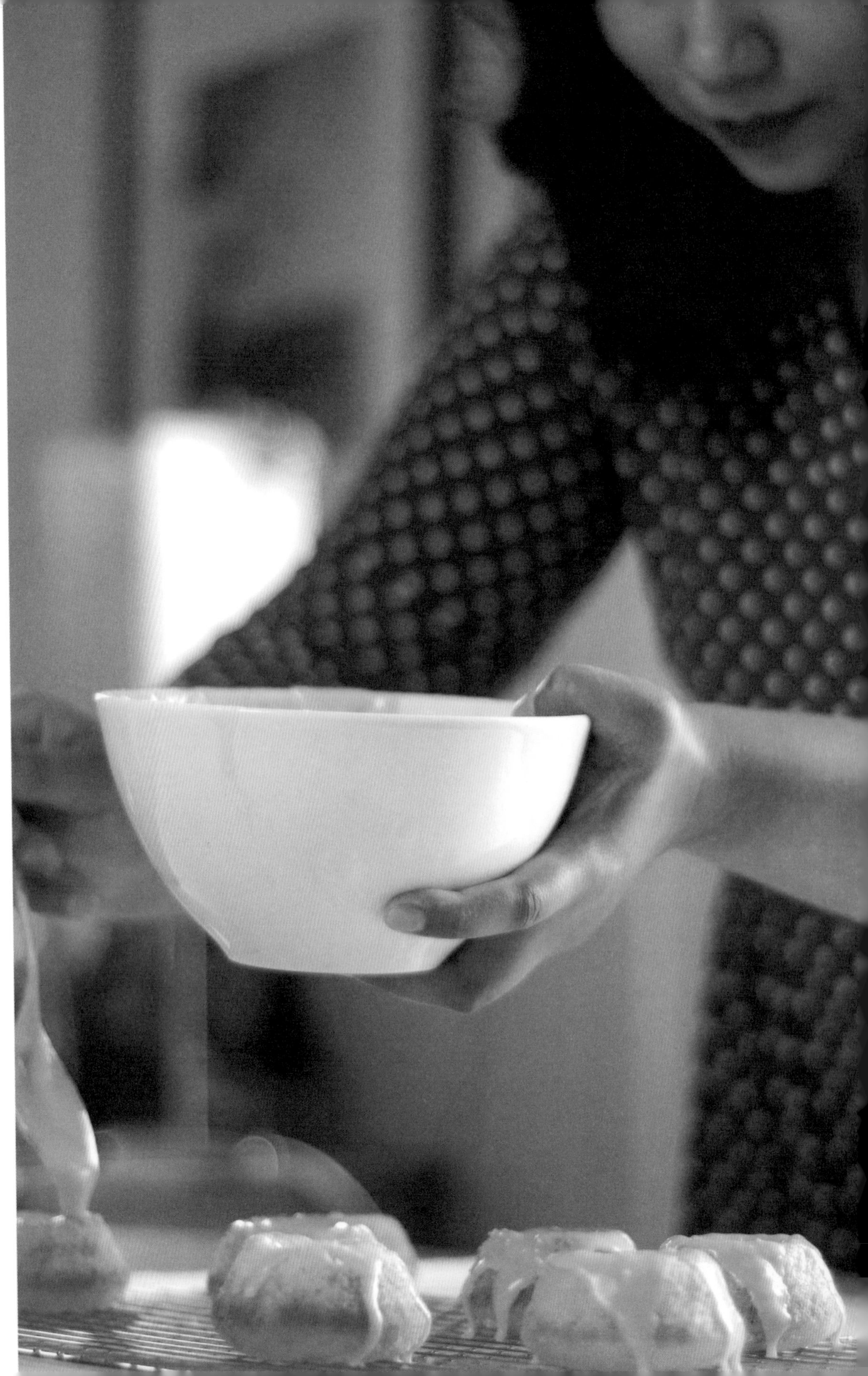

RAW COFFEE BROWNIE
Gluten-free/dairy-free/soy-free/
vegan/vegetarian/nobake/paleo/sugar-free

Gluten-free oats,
cashews, dates, cacao, coconut, coffee
3.50

RAW PALEO
COFFEE BROWNIE

ST SUGAR OF
LONDON
STREET FOOD
MARKET

Makes 16
V, WF, GF

Enzo at St Sugar of London has the best baking and some great slogans like 'let them eat brioche' and 'zero grains zero sugar for an unfattable planet'. This raw coffee brownie is one of his 'zero grains zero sugar' treats so you're onto a winner: rich and indulgent, it is also super healthy and nutritious. It's a completely raw recipe and requires very little processing in line with paleo philosophy. The taste relies on the quality of the ingredients, so for best results use organic – the cacao, coffee and coconut oil should be the best you can buy.

125g unsalted cashews
250g pitted dates
30g cacao powder
125g gluten-free oats
½–1 tablespoon ground coffee
½ tablespoon coconut oil
sea salt

20cm square tin

Soak the cashews and dates in cold water overnight, then drain and blend to a smooth paste. If you have a powerful food processor, you can skip the soaking and grind the nuts from dry, then add the dates and blend to a paste. Scrape the paste into a mixing bowl. Add the cacao, oats, ground coffee and a pinch of sea salt.

Gently melt the coconut oil in a bain-marie: boil some water in a small pan and put the coconut oil in a heatproof bowl that sits on top of the pan. Stir carefully until melted. Take the coconut oil off the heat and mix into the cashew mixture to make a thick dough. For a rougher textured brownie (closer to an energy bar) just do this by hand; for a smoother, more fudgy result use a food processor.

Press the mixture into your tin with the back of a spoon and put into the fridge to solidify overnight. You can also freeze the brownies – just defrost, then cut into little squares and serve.

CARDAMOM SHORTBREAD

Makes 12 slices
EF

Shortbread is a quintessentially British biscuit: rich, buttery and crumbly and perfect with a cup of tea. I've given this recipe an Eastern twist with the addition of fragrant cardamom – easily my favourite spice. After all, Brick Lane is the place where East meets West. These not only look pleasing to the eye, but they also taste delicious.

150g unsalted butter,
  at room temperature
65g caster sugar, plus more
  for sprinkling
½ teaspoon freshly
  ground cardamom
150g plain flour
40g rice flour
⅛ teaspoon salt

20cm round baking tin

Place the butter into a mixing bowl with the sugar and cardamom and cream together for three to four minutes until pale and fluffy. Tip in the flour, rice flour and salt and mix with a wooden spoon until it comes together into a dough. You may need to use your hand to complete forming the dough but make sure you do this quickly so as not to make the dough greasy from your body heat.

Press the dough evenly into the baking tin with the back of a spoon. There's no need to grease the pan as the mixture is already very buttery. Go around the edges of the dough pinching gently with your thumb and forefinger, creating a decorative rim. Score into 12 portions as you would slice a cake, then put in the fridge and chill for 20 minutes. Preheat your oven to 160°C (140°C fan).

Sprinkle generously with some caster sugar and bake for 45 to 55 minutes, or until golden all over but not browned. Cool completely in the tin, then turn out onto a wooden board to slice. The shortbread round should come out from the tin easily but if not, go very gently around the edges with a thin knife, place one palm on the front and flip it out. Slice into the 12 scored portions with a sharp knife to serve. The shortbread keeps well for a few days in an airtight container.

VEGAN BAKLAVA

The Boiler House food hall houses Gozleme, this wonderful vegetarian and vegan street food stall, and I was surprised to see they had veganised one of my favourite Turkish desserts. Gozleme's version is perfect if you avoid dairy and want to limit your refined sugar: the syrup is partly made with agave syrup, a lovely natural sweetener. Baklava is very sweet so this recipe will satisfy a big group – great served as petits fours at a gathering. Most commonly available filo pastry brands are vegan but check before you buy.

FOR THE BAKLAVA:

200g walnuts

1 teaspoon ground cinnamon

250g dairy free margarine
  (such as Vitalite)

35 sheets vegan filo pastry

FOR THE SYRUP:

220g sugar

100ml agave syrup

juice of ½ lemon

5 cloves

26cm x 20cm baking tin

Preheat your oven to 220°C (200°C fan).

Finely chop the walnuts in a food processor, then add the cinnamon. Melt the margarine in a small pan. Place a sheet of filo in the baking tin, then brush with melted margarine and repeat until you have a base of ten brushed sheets.

Spread a quarter of the walnut and cinnamon mixture in a layer on top and cover with five more sheets of pastry, brushing each with the margarine as you go. Make three more layers of walnuts, each separated by five sheets of filo pastry. Cover the final layer of walnuts with ten sheets of filo, each brushed with margarine apart from the very top one.

Using a sharp knife, slice the baklava into small diamonds or squares, then brush the top with margarine and put in the oven. Bake for 18 to 20 minutes, until golden and crisp on top.

About ten minutes before the baklava is ready, prepare the syrup. Place the sugar, agave syrup, lemon juice and cloves in a pan with 230ml water. Simmer over medium-low heat for four or five minutes until small bubbles appear over the surface and you have a light syrup. Remove the cloves.

Take the baklava out of the oven and pour the hot syrup evenly over it. Leave to cool and absorb the syrup before serving.

BAKED CHEESECAKE

BEIGEL SHOP
155 BRICK LANE

Serves 12

A trip to Brick Lane is incomplete without a slice of baked cheesecake from Beigel Shop, and this recipe is based on their best-selling dessert. The thick, creamy cheese filling with a hint of vanilla and lemon sits on top of a thin biscuit base with an almost imperceptible almond taste. It's simply delicious as is, so there's no need to add any sauces or toppings.

100g digestive biscuits
50g rich tea biscuits
60g butter, at room temperature
¼ teaspoon almond extract
400g cream cheese
200g caster sugar
150ml soured cream
100ml double cream
4 medium eggs
juice of ½ lemon
vanilla extract
2 tablespoons cornflour

23cm springform cake tin

Preheat your oven to 170°C (150°C fan). Grease the tin and line the sides with a strip of greaseproof paper.

Whiz the biscuits into fine crumbs in a food processor (or put them into a ziplock bag and bash with a rolling pin). Melt the butter in a small pan over medium heat, then stir in the biscuit crumbs and almond extract. Press the mixture firmly into the base of the prepared cake tin and bake for ten minutes. Remove from the oven and cool. Whisk together the cream cheese and sugar, then add the soured cream, double cream and the eggs and blend together until smooth and fluffy – this will take two to three minutes with an electric whisk, or about five minutes by hand. Mix in the lemon juice, vanilla extract and cornflour and mix again until everything is combined.

Pour the mixture into the tin and bake for 60 to 90 minutes. The surface will be puffy and light golden. Leave in the oven for 30 minutes with the door ajar and then cool completely at room temperature. Chill in the fridge for three to four hours before serving.

Chef's tip – to avoid a cracked surface it is essential that you leave the cheesecake in the oven with the door ajar for at least 30 minutes.

CHOCOLATE-DIPPED STRAWBERRIES IN OREO CRUMBS

CHOCO FRUIT
SUNDAY
UPMARKET

Serves 4
EF, WF, GF

I'd been following Choco Fruit on social media for a while and always loved seeing their bright and colourful chocolate-covered fruit creations. So when David kindly shared this recipe for his wonderful chocolate strawberry skewers with me, I was in a huge rush to get to my test kitchen and try it for myself. I've since spent many moments salivating over this simple but ingenious, almost no-cook treat. It delivers your chocolate hit *and* one of your five a day! What's not to love?

300g fresh strawberries
1 pack Oreo biscuits
500g Belgian chocolate coins
2½ tablespoons butter

4 x 20cm wooden skewers

Hull your strawberries and wash in warm water, then drain off in a colander. Put the Oreo biscuits in a bowl and crush to crumbs with the end of a rolling pin. Place your chocolate coins in a microwavable dish along with the butter, and put in the microwave for about four to six minutes on maximum heat. Keep a close eye on the mixture, stirring occasionally, and stop when everything is melted and smooth.

Dip your strawberries one by one into your melted chocolate. Place them a centimetre apart on greaseproof paper, then sprinkle with the crushed Oreo crumbs and leave to set. Once the chocolate is hard, put five strawberries on each skewer and serve, much to everyone's delight.

ITALIAN BLUEBERRY CHEESECAKE

ENOTECA POMAIO
224 BRICK LANE

Serves 4

This is an easy no-bake cheesecake recipe, Italian-style. Delicious almond cantucci biscuits are crumbled and layered with ricotta vanilla custard and swirls of sweet blueberry jam – it's all good but it's the whipped ricotta custard that makes me keep coming back for more.

200ml whole milk
200ml single cream
1 vanilla pod, split lengthways
80g sugar
4 medium egg yolks
1 teaspoon plain flour, sifted
1 teaspoon cornflour, sifted
300g ricotta cheese
150g cantucci biscuits,
  ground to fine crumbs
200g blueberry jam

Place the milk, cream and vanilla pod in a pan with 40 grams of the sugar and bring to a boil, whisking until the sugar dissolves. Turn off the heat. In a bowl, whisk the egg yolks with the remaining sugar, flour and cornflour to form a smooth paste.

Discard the vanilla pod from the warm cream mixture, then slowly pour it onto the eggs, whisking constantly so they don't scramble. Once everything is combined, pour back into the pan. Turn the heat to medium-high and keep whisking for two or three minutes until you have a thick custard. Take off the heat and cool completely.

When the custard has cooled, add the ricotta cheese and whip with a whisk until you have a smooth cream. Now, in four individual serving bowls or one larger dish, assemble your cheesecake. Alternate layers of cantucci biscuit crumbs, blueberry jam and the cheese cream mixture until you use up all the ingredients.

Serve at room temperature or chilled.

MAHALLABI
SYRIAN MILK PUDDING

DAMASCU BITE
119–121
BRICK LANE

Serves 6
WF, GF, EF

Chef Abu Mouaz kindly contributed this special Syrian milk pudding, made with cornflour and traditionally eaten at weddings and during the winter months. It's a light and delicate dish and makes me think of a Middle Eastern panna cotta – fragrant with rosewater, with a little bit of salt to bring out the sweetness (according to Abu). It may seem very simple to make, but believe me when I say that is simply exquisite, especially when topped with whipped cream, fresh fruits and chopped nuts. You can also serve it with a vibrant rosewater syrup (page 200) which I think works really well.

1 litre whole milk

6 tablespoons sugar

6 tablespoons cornflour

¼ teaspoon salt

1 tablespoon rosewater

6 individual dishes

Put six tablespoons of the milk in a small bowl and pour the rest into a deep pan. Put the pan over a high heat until the milk is hot but not boiling, then turn it down to medium. Whisk the sugar, cornflour and salt with the reserved milk, then add to the pan, whisking constantly to prevent lumps forming. Keep whisking for four or five minutes until the mahallabi is the consistency of thick custard. Add the rosewater and pour into six individual dishes (or one large one) to cool.

Once the mahallabi is cool, chill in the refrigerator. To serve, pour over some rosewater syrup or top with whipped cream, pistachios, almonds and fresh fruit – in the summer I like a mix of cherries and strawberries.

ROSEWATER SYRUP

Serves 4-6
V, WF, GF

This syrup is inspired by the mahallabi recipe from Abu at Damascu Bite. Syrups are a great way to add some flavour to a variety of sweet dishes and this rose syrup is perfect with or without a pink hue. It's not just good on mahallabi – I use it to top yoghurts and puddings and it's also great poured over pancakes, or brushed onto warm cakes for added moisture.

150g sugar
2 teaspoons lime juice
1 tablespoon rosewater
drop of pink food colour
 (optional)

Put the sugar and lime juice in a pan with 200ml water and bring to the boil. Simmer gently on medium heat for five minutes until you have a light syrup. Turn off the heat, then add the rosewater and food colouring (if using) and stir through. Cool completely before serving. The syrup stores well for up to a week in the fridge.

COCONUT & JAGGERY KHEER
RICE PUDDING

Serves 4-6
WF, GF, EF

Rice pudding means comfort food and this version is not just comforting but warm and fragrant and rich. It's based on my mum's recipe and is flavoured with a little coconut and the lovely caramel sweetness of jaggery. An added bonus is that it's easily veganised – just switch the whole milk for coconut or almond milk. A perfect ending to an Asian meal.

100g basmati rice, soaked for
  an hour and drained
1 litre whole milk
50g desiccated coconut
150g jaggery, crumbled
6 cardamom pods,
  lightly crushed
1 stick cinnamon
1 bay leaf

Add the soaked rice to a large saucepan and bring to the boil with 500ml water. Simmer on medium heat for five minutes and then add the milk, coconut, jaggery, cardamom pods, cinnamon and bay leaf and bring back to the boil.

Reduce the heat to a medium and simmer and stir continuously for 30 to 40 minutes, until the rice is cooked and broken up and the milk has reduced by almost half. Serve hot or chilled, topped with nuts or toasted coconut.

PISTACHIO & VANILLA CRÈME BRÛLÉE

CHEZ ELLES
45 BRICK LANE

Serves 4
WF, GF

Chez Elles' pistachio and vanilla crème brûlée is to die for. Nadia kindly gave me this recipe which I secretly hoped she wouldn't want to keep secret! The pudding is rich, thick and decadent and the pistachio paste gives almost macaron-like flavour. Most crème brûlée recipes involve making a custard first; however this method couldn't be simpler: everything is simply whisked together before being baked, then finished with that distinctive crunchy, sugary topping. You can get pistachio paste online from Sous Chef (www.souschef.co.uk).

60g sugar, plus 6 teaspoons
  for caramelising
4 egg yolks
½ vanilla pod
15g pistachio paste
125ml whole milk
375ml double cream

4 ramekins
blow torch (optional)

Preheat your oven to 140°C (120°C fan). In a mixing bowl, whisk together 60 grams of sugar and the egg yolks with an electric mixer until the sugar has dissolved. Scrape the seeds from the vanilla pod and add to the mix along with the pistachio paste. Whisk to combine, then add the milk and cream and keep whisking everything together for a few minutes until the mixture is foamy.

Sieve the mix and divide between four ramekins. Place the ramekins in a deep roasting tin and place into the oven. Once the tin is in the oven, fill it with water to about halfway up the sides of the ramekins and bake for an hour. They'll still be very wobbly in the middle, but set them aside to cool and they'll firm up nicely. Once completely cool, chill in the fridge.

Sprinkle each pudding with one and a half teaspoons of sugar and gently shake the ramekins to make an even layer. Caramelise the tops using a blow torch or place under a very hot grill for a couple of minutes. Using the grill takes a little longer so keep turning the ramekins to make sure they brown evenly.

ROSHGOLLA
SWEET MILK DUMPLINGS IN SYRUP

Alauddin's rich history spans over a century. The original store opened in Dhaka, Bangladesh in 1894 and was founded by a Mr Alauddin of Alauddin Halwai, who arrived from Lucknow in India, famous for its sweet-making. In the 1980s, the company opened their first UK outposts and the Brick Lane store opened in 1990. It soon became a firm favourite amongst locals with its menu of authentic sweetmeats. Roshgolla are one of their best sellers: milk curd dumplings, rolled into smooth balls, then boiled in a light syrup until they absorb the syrup and swell up. A delicious and classic Bengali dessert, these are best served the day they are cooked.

FOR THE DUMPLINGS:

1 litre whole milk

2–3 tablespoons vinegar
   or lemon juice

1 teaspoon plain flour

FOR THE SYRUP:

225g sugar

muslin cloth or fine tea towel

Place the milk in a large non-stick pan and bring to a boil. Reduce the heat to a gentle simmer and add the vinegar or lemon juice. Stir briefly with a wooden spoon until the milk curd separates from the whey. Turn off the flame. Line a colander with a muslin cloth or fine tea towel and put it in the sink. Carefully pour the contents of the pan into the colander, then gently rinse the milk curd several times with cold water to remove any acidic flavour.

Twist the tops of the cloth together and squeeze out any excess liquid. Tie the tops of the cloth on the tap and let it hang over your sink for at least 30 minutes to an hour. Squeeze again to make sure all excess water has drained out and place the curds on a dry dish. If the mixture seems damp at all spread it over a tray and leave for another 30 minutes to dry out – if the roshgollas aren't dry enough they will fall apart in the syrup.

Make your syrup by placing the sugar in a medium-sized pan with 250ml water. Bring to the boil and cook on high heat for five minutes. Turn the heat down to very low while you prepare the curd dumplings.

Add the flour to the dried curds and knead very well with the heel of your hands until smooth – this will take around five minutes. You will know when it's ready as your palm will feel ever so slightly greasy. Divide into eight equal portions and roll into smooth balls between your palms. Now carefully drop the balls into the syrup and simmer on low heat for five minutes – you'll see the balls expanding slightly. Carefully turn each one over and increase heat to medium. Cover and cook for another 20 minutes, until the roshogollas almost double in size. Carefully transfer to a heatproof dish and pour the remaining syrup on top. Leave to cool for at least two or three hours before serving at room temperature.

alauddin
sweets & rest
New Chillies
www.chilliesuk.com
RESTAURANT
020 7247 7539
THE MONSOON
OPEN TILL LATE
OON
OPEN TILL LATE
020 7377 0896
alauddin sweets
alauddin sweets
alauddin
swee

KALOJAAM
DEEP-FRIED DUMPLINGS IN SYRUP

ALAUDDIN SWEETS
72 BRICK LANE

Makes 8
EF

At Alauddin, traditional sweet-making methods are preserved by skilled artisans from Dhaka and the famous Bengali desert Kalojaam is another of their bestsellers. Soft pieces of fried dough are immersed in a light syrup and cooked until you are left with soft, caramel-flavoured dumplings. The exterior of this croquette-shaped sweet is almost *kalo* (or black in Bengali) and the interior is traditionally deep red or pink, resembling *jaam*, a berry-like fruit popular in Bangladesh. To avoid sweet-making mishaps, make sure you use full cream milk powder – ideally Nido brand which can be found in Asian grocers.

FOR THE DUMPLINGS:

200g full cream milk powder

25g plain flour

⅛ teaspoon bicarbonate
  of soda

small drop of red food colouring

1 tablespoon ghee

5 tablespoons whole milk

350ml vegetable oil,
  for deep frying

FOR THE SYRUP:

450g sugar

In a bowl, mix together the milk powder, plain flour, bicarbonate of soda, food colouring and ghee and crumble together with your fingertips. Add the milk and knead for seven or eight minutes until you have a soft, smooth dough. Divide into eight pieces and roll each one into a slightly elongated croquette shape.

Prepare the syrup: put the sugar in a pan with 500ml water on medium heat. The pan should be smallish and not too wide – you need the syrup to be deep enough so that the sweets can be fully submerged in it. Bring the syrup to the boil and simmer for five minutes, then turn off the heat and set aside while you fry the sweets.

Heat the oil in a deep frying pan or wok on medium-high heat. You can check it's hot enough for cooking the kalojaam by dropping a small piece of bread into the oil. If is sizzles to the surface the oil is ready. Once hot, reduce the heat to low and gently slide four of the kalojaam pieces into the oil. They will double in size as they cook, so ensure that there is enough room for them to expand. Fry for five minutes or so until the kalojaam are very dark brown all over – make sure they colour evenly by gently moving them around occasionally with a fork. Repeat with the remaining four kalojaam.

When the kalojaam are almost done, turn the heat back on the syrup and bring to a simmer. Add the fried kalojaam to the syrup and cook for ten minutes. Remove them one by one from the syrup and place in a serving dish. Pour the hot syrup over the top and cool. Serve at room temperature, or chilled.

FLAMBÉ COGNAC TRUFFLES

DARK SUGARS
141 BRICK LANE

Makes about 45
EF, WF, GF

The finest handmade chocolate shop in the East End is chock-a-block with small mountains of truffles and pralines as well as divine hot chocolates topped with yet more shaved chocolate! So when the owner, Fatou, agreed to give me the recipe for their signature flambé truffles, I was over the moon – you cannot beat these for decadent petits fours or handmade gifts. Just be sure to use very good quality chocolate. The recipe makes about 45 truffles – it sounds a lot but you can make a batch with half of the ganache and freeze the remainder for another occasion. These are best made the day before serving as the mixture needs to rest.

300ml double cream
500g plain chocolate
  (min. 70% cocoa solids),
  finely chopped
125ml cognac
100g cocoa powder

Put the cream in a saucepan and set on medium-low heat. Bring to the boil, then take the saucepan off the heat and add the chocolate. Stir very gently until the chocolate has completely melted into the cream. To flambé or flame the cognac, pour it into a small saucepan and put over a medium-low heat. Warm it until bubbles start to form at the side of the pan, then light it with a long match and take off the heat immediately. Let the alcohol burn off, keeping a saucepan lid handy to put out the flames once they turn from blue to yellow, as they can get quite high! Stir the cognac into the chocolate mixture until it's combined. Place the ganache in the fridge for at least three or four hours and preferably overnight. Bring the ganache out of the fridge and scoop out teaspoonfuls, rolling them lightly into balls between your palms.

At Dark Sugars they dip the truffles in tempered chocolate and then into cocoa powder. At home, I like to roll them straight in the cocoa powder. Either way, put them in the fridge for at least 15 minutes before serving.

Strawberry, Banana & Mango smoothie
£2.50

Passion Fruit & Mango Smoothie
£2.50

Mix Berries,James & Mango Smoothie
£2.50

DRINKS
DRINKS
DRINKS
DRINKS

CHOCOLATE CHAI

Serves 4
WF, GF, EF

My twist on the classic masala chai recipe. The addition of chocolate makes it even more of a treat and with added whipped cream you might even call it a spiced hot chocolate. I like mine fairly sweet but you can adjust the sugar according to your taste.

8 cardamom pods

1 stick cinnamon

4 cloves

4 peppercorns

2cm fresh ginger, peeled
  and sliced

4 teaspoons loose black tea
  (or 4 tea bags)

500ml whole milk

2–3 tablespoons sugar

2 tablespoons unsweetened
  cocoa powder

In a pan bring 600ml water to the boil. Using a pestle and mortar, lightly crush the cardamom, cinnamon, cloves, peppercorns and ginger, then add them to the pan and simmer on medium heat for three minutes. Add the tea and simmer for a further two minutes, then pour in the milk. Bring back to the boil, and turn the heat to low.

In a small bowl, mix the sugar and cocoa powder to a paste with a tablespoon of cold water, then add it to the pan. Simmer for another minute or two, then taste and adjust the sweetness if necessary. Strain into cups and serve – with some whipped cream and a sprinkle of cinnamon if you're feeling particularly indulgent.

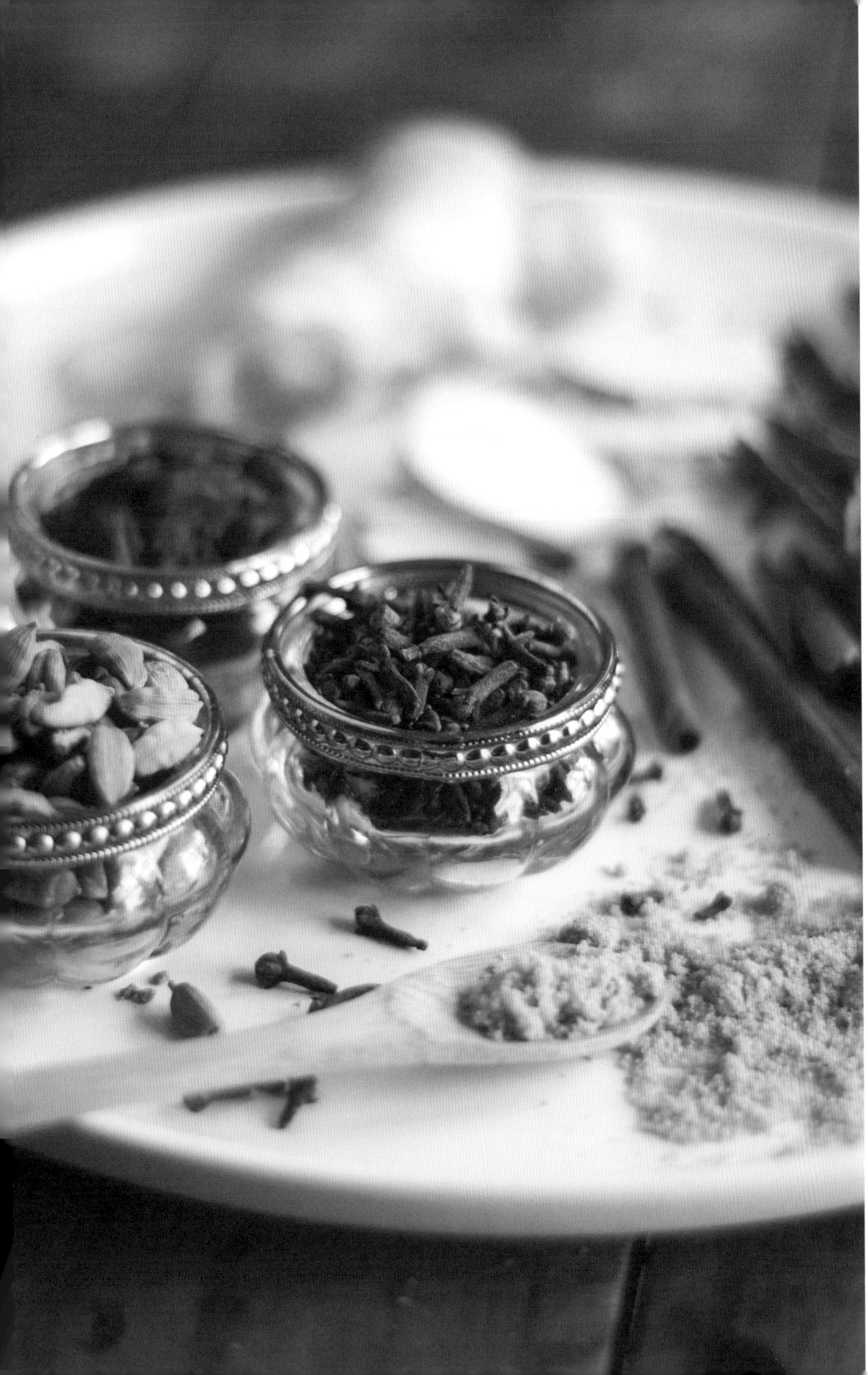

EASY VIETNAMESE
ICED COFFEE

Serves 2
EF, WF, GF

One of my favourite drinks is sweet, milky iced coffee and it doesn't get better than this. I know this is the cheat's version but I was inspired by Eat Chay, one of the Vietnamese traders in Brick Lane, and had to try it at home. This is so easy to make with a cafetière or stovetop coffee maker if you don't have a traditional Vietnamese coffee filter: you basically make two cups of espresso and pour them into sweetened condensed milk. A great pick me up for when you're having one of those days.

6 tablespoons sweetened
 condensed milk
200ml freshly brewed espresso
8 ice cubes

First make some freshly brewed espresso, so that you have about 100ml coffee per serving. Put three tablespoons of condensed milk into each of two heatproof serving glasses and top with the espresso. Stir, then add four ice cubes to each glass and serve.

CHAI-NA GIRL
SUPERCHARGED SMOOTHIE

STAY TROPICAL
BOILER HOUSE FOOD
HALL

Serves 2
V, GF, WF

Stay Tropical are market traders with a difference: a plastic-free, environmentally inclined social enterprise, they sell delicious, 100% natural energising smoothies and donate 25% of all their profits to rainforest protection. For each smoothie sold, they give a drink to somebody who is homeless. Company founder Jamie first discovered the amazing flavours used in this Chai-Na Girl recipe while travelling around India in 2006. When he started trading at Brick Lane he was determined to invent something using this utterly delicious concoction of spices. Instead of tea, he subbed in some cold brew coffee for an extra kick that really supercharges the smoothie, and the result is now is one of his bestsellers. The chai spice mix makes enough for four servings, so keep the leftovers in an airtight container.

FOR THE SMOOTHIE:

1 frozen banana

2 Medjool dates

200ml Rocketman cold brew
  coffee (or any good coffee)

500ml coconut milk

2 teaspoons chai spice mix

2 teaspoons agave syrup

2 ice cubes

CHAI SPICE MIX:

1 teaspoon cardamon

1 teaspoon allspice

2 teaspoons ground cinnamon

1 teaspoon ground cloves

3 teaspoon ground ginger

Jamie's methods are simple – chuck everything in a blender, mix it up, and enjoy!

MANGO & CARDAMOM LASSI

Serves 4
GF, WF, EF

Childhood trips to Brick Lane on Sunday morning usually involved grocery shopping and browsing the various wares set up on the stalls – clothes, ornate bits of costume jewellery and crates and crates of fresh fruit and vegetables. One of the highlights was of course lunch at Sweet & Spicy, which always included refreshing glasses of lassi served from an aluminium pitcher. If you can get hold of Pakistani Chaunsa or Indian Kesar mangoes in the Asian grocery stores, then they are the best to use (they both have a very short season in early summer). The rest of the year, use Brazilian mangos which are readily available but not as sweet, so you'll need to add a little more sugar.

2 very ripe Pakistani or Indian mangoes, peeled and roughly chopped
500g Greek yoghurt
⅔ teaspoon ground cardamom
250ml milk
4–6 tablespoons sugar

Place the mango pieces in a blender or smoothie maker (you can also use a hand blender) and add the yogurt and cardamom. Blitz together for about 30 seconds, then add the milk and sugar and blitz for another minute until the lassi is creamy and smooth. I suggest you add a tablespoon of sugar per person as you begin, and adjust according to taste.

A glass of lassi is best enjoyed chilled and is so good with samosas or pakoras.

STRAWBERRY & ROSE LASSI

Serves 4
WF, GF, EF

Inspired by Indian summers by way of East London, this makes an interesting twist on the classic warm weather treat. I like to serve this with a mezze of Middle Eastern and Indian small plates. Use very ripe strawberries and adjust the rosewater according to taste – you're looking for a lovely floral note without it being too overpowering. This lassi isn't meant to be as thick as the mango version but is a lighter, more refreshing experience.

400g strawberries, hulled
150ml milk
500g Greek yogurt
4–6 tablespoons honey
1½ tablespoons rosewater

Place the strawberries, milk and yoghurt in the blender and blitz until smooth. Add four tablespoons of honey and the rosewater and blitz again. Taste and add more honey if it needs more sweetness. Serve chilled.

INDEX

X

Y

Z

BRICK LANE